PS
3545
A748
A795   72-1948

dies
in
Men

DATE DUE

CHARLES E. MERRILL STUDIES

Under the General Editorship of
Matthew J. Bruccoli and Joseph Katz

The Merrill Studies
in
All the King's Men

Compiled by
James F. Light
University of Bridgeport

Charles E. Merrill Publishing Company
A Bell & Howell Company
Columbus, Ohio

ISBN: 0-675-09197-7

Library of Congress Number: 78-153293

1 2 3 4 5 6 7 8 9 — 79 78 77 76 75 74 73 72 71

Printed in the United States of America

Preface

Born in Kentucky in 1905, Robert Penn Warren spent his early life in the South, graduated from Vanderbilt University (*summa cum laude*) in 1925, and then pursued graduate studies at Yale and Oxford. A Rhodes Scholar, he received the B. Litt. degree from Oxford in 1930, after which he set out on a joint career as teacher and author. As a writer he has published significant work in a variety of literary forms: eight novels, one play, numerous short stories and critical essays, three influential literary texts, a biography of John Brown, nine volumes of poetry, and three volumes of social analysis of American race relations. The distinction of his work has brought him numerous honors. Twice he has been awarded Guggenheim Fellowships, and he is the only writer to have won Pulitzer prizes in both fiction(for *All the King's Men*, 1946) and poetry (for *Promises*, 1957). In 1967 he was awarded The Bollingen Prize for Poetry for his *Selected Poems: New and Old, 1923-1966*; in 1969 he received the Van Wyck Brooks Award for *belles lettres* for his volume of poems entitled *Audubon*; and in 1970 he was awarded the National Medal for Literature as a recognition of his total contribution to the world of letters. Numerous universities have awarded him honorary degrees.

Quite possibly, however, Warren's highest artistic achievement has been in fiction, and there is fairly general agreement that *All the King's Men* is the best of his novels. In it, Warren reveals, as completely as in anything he has written, the vitality of his talent and the breadth of his mind. In the novel he shows his fondness for philosophic and theological speculation and illuminates his leanings towards what he calls impure poetry which is based on robust reality but also exhibits a considerable fondness for lyric language, allusive images, and symbolic motifs. The novel's indictment of mechanism and industrialism reveals Warren's partial kinship with the Nashville group of writers called the fugitives (because of their association with the magazine *The Fugitive*) who romanticized agrarianism and the Southern way of life. In the novel's delineation of a historical milieu, in its concern for the complicated problems of social justice, in its obsession with man's need to know, no matter whether knowledge may save him or damn him, Warren reveals his intense concern for the human predicament.

More than anything else, however, *All the King's Men* is the product of a skillful artist. Warren not only tells his tale with consummate craftsmanship (the first chapter is brilliant in its mechanistic imagery, in its contrast between the settings of the social classes, and in its foreshadowing of the novel's action as a whole), but also captures the Grecian inevitability and the human universality of two good men — though good in different ways — who are destroyed by tragic flaws in their characters. Like Melville's Ishmael, whom he resembles in a number of ways, Jack Burden seems left alone at the end of the novel to proclaim after the general destruction: "And I alone am escaped to tell thee."

In the first part of this collection of materials relevant to the study of *All the King's Men* I have attempted to illuminate a few of the varying biographical, philosophical, and literary sources of the novel. In doing so I hope the relationship of the novel to a particular moment in history, as well as to some universal historical dilemmas, may be clarified. Students of history should certainly be able to draw parallels between Willie Stark (no matter how much or how little he may have been inspired by Huey Long) and other dictatorial types, from Caesar and Caligula to Hitler, Mussolini, and Stalin.

In the second part of the collection I have presented selections which, I hope, clarify the novel itself while also revealing examples of various critical approaches to literature; these range from an early review of the novel (Davis), to discussions of the novel in the context of Warren's literary art (Anderson), the method of explication of the single text alone (Light), and to examples of such various critical perspectives as the sociological (Sillars), the mythological (White), and the theological (Ruoff). The rays of light thrown from these different angles of vision do not, of course, illuminate the entirety of the novel, and individual teachers may well prefer to approach the novel from an entirely different perspective than any of those illustrated. The complexity of the thought and the depth of the artistry of the novel are partially implied by the fact that it is so rewarding to so many different readers.

JFL

Contents

1. Some Sources

A. Biographical

B. Philosophical

C. Literary

2. Varied Critical Approaches

A. An Early Review

B. The Novel in Context

C. Explication de Texte

D. From a Sociological Perspective

E. From a Mythological Perspective

F. From a Theological Perspective

1. Some Sources

Robert Penn Warren

All The King's Men:
The Matrix of Experience

When I am asked how much *All the King's Men* owes to the actual politics of Louisiana in the '30's, I can only be sure that if I had never gone to live in Louisiana and if Huey Long had not existed, the novel would never have been written. But this is far from saying that my "state" in *All the King's Men* is Louisiana (or any of the other forty-nine stars in our flag), or that my Willie Stark is the late Senator. What Louisiana and Senator Long gave me was a line of thinking and feeling that did eventuate in the novel.

In the summer of 1934 I was offered a job — a much-needed job — as Assistant Professor at the Louisiana State University, in Baton Rouge. It was "Huey Long's University," and definitely on the make — with a sensational football team and with money to spend even for assistant professors at a time when assistant professors were being fired, not hired — as I knew all too well. It was Huey's University, but he, I was assured, would never mess with my classroom. That was to prove true; he was far too adept in the arts of power to care what an assistant professor might have to say. The only time that his presence was ever felt in my classroom was when, in my Shakespeare course, I gave my little annual lecture on the political background of *Julius Caesar;* and then, for the two weeks we spent on the play, backs grew straighter, eyes grew brighter, notes were taken, and the girls stopped knitting in class, or repairing their faces.

In September 1934 I left Tennessee, where I had been living on a farm near Nashville, drove down across Mississippi, crossed the river by ferry (where I can't be sure — was it at Greenville?) and was in North Louisiana. Along the way I picked up a hitch-hiker — a country man, the kind you call a redneck or a wool-hat, aging, aimless, nondescript, beat up by life and hard times and bad luck; clearly tooth-broke and probably gut-shot, standing beside the road in an attitude that spoke of infinite patience

Reprinted from *Yale Review*, LIII (Winter, 1964), 161-67, by permission of the William Morris Agency. Copyright © 1964 by Robert Penn Warren.

and considerable fortitude, holding a parcel in his hand, wrapped in old newspaper and tied with binder twine, waiting for some car to come along. He was, though at the moment I did not sense it, a mythological figure.

He was the god on the battlement, dimly perceived above the darkling tumult and the streaming carnage of the political struggle. He was a voice, a portent, and a natural force like the Mississippi River getting set to bust a levee. Long before the Fascist March on Rome, Norman Douglas, meditating on Naples, had predicted that the fetid slums of Europe would make possible the "inspired idiot." His predictive diagnosis of the origins of fascism — and of communism — may be incomplete, but it is certain that the rutted back roads and slab-side shacks that had spawned my nameless old hitchhiker, with the twine-tied paper parcel in his hand, had, by that fall of 1934, made possible the rise of "Huey." My nameless hitchhiker was, mythologically speaking, Long's *sine qua non.*

So it was appropriate that he should tell me the first episode of the many I had to hear of the myth that was "Huey." The roads, he said, was shore better now. A man could git to market, he said. A man could jist git up and git, if'n a notion come on him. Did'n have to pay no toll at no toll bridge neither. Fer Huey was a free-bridge man. So he went on and told me how, standing on the river bank by a toll bridge (by what river and what bridge was never clear), Huey had made the president of the company that owned the bridge a good, fair cash offer, and the man laughed at him. But, the old hitchhiker said, Huey did'n do nothing but lean over and pick him up a chunk of rock and throwed it off a-ways, and asked did that president-feller see whar the rock hit. The feller said yeah, he seen. Wal, Huey said, the next thing you see is gonna be a big new free bridge right whar that rock hit, and you, you son-of-a-bitch, are goen bankrupt a-ready and doan even know it.

There were a thousand tales, over the years, and some of them were, no doubt, literally and factually true. But they were all true in the world of "Huey" — that world of myth, folklore, poetry, deprivation, rancor, and dimly envisaged hopes. That world had a strange, shifting, often ironical and sometimes irrelevant relation to the factual world of Senator Huey P. Long and his cold manipulation of the calculus of power. The two worlds, we may hazard, merged only at the moment when in September 1935, in the corridor of the Capitol, the little .32 slug bit meanly into the senatorial vitals.

There was another world — this a factual world — made possible by the factual Long, though not inhabited by him. It was a world that I, as an assistant professor, was to catch fleeting glimpses of, and ponder. It was the world of the parasites of power, a world that Long was, apparently, contemptuous of, but knew how to use, as he knew how to use other things of which he was, perhaps, contemptuous. This was a world of a sick yearning for elegance and the sight of one's name on the society page of a New Orleans paper; it was the world of the electric moon devised, it was alleged, to cast a romantic glow over the garden when the President of the University and his wife entertained their politicos and pseudo-socialites; it was a world of pretentiousness, of blood-curdling struggles for academic preferment, of drool-jawed grab and arrogant criminality. It was a world all too suggestive, in its small-bore, provincial way, of the airs and aspirations that the newspapers attributed to that ex-champagne salesman Von Ribbentrop and to the inner circle of Edda Ciano's friends.

For in Louisiana, in the 1930's, you felt somehow that you were living in the great world, or at least in a microcosm with all the forces and fatalities faithfully, if sometimes comically, drawn to scale. And the little Baton Rouge world of campus and Governor's Mansion and Capitol and the gold bathroom fixtures reported to be in the house of the University contractor was, once the weight of Long's contempt and political savvy had been removed by the bullet of the young Brutus in the Capitol, to plunge idiotically rampant to an end almost as dramatic as the scenes in the last bunkers of Berlin or at the filling station on the outskirts of Milan. The headlines advertised the suicides, and the population of penitentiaries, both Federal and state, received some distinguished additions.

But this is getting ahead of the story. Meanwhile, there was, besides the lurid worlds, the world of ordinary life to look at. There were the people who ran stores or sold insurance or had a farm and tried to survive and pay their debts. There were —visible even from the new concrete speedway that Huey had slashed through the cypress swamps toward New Orleans — the palmetto-leaf and sheet-iron hovels of the moss pickers, rising like some fungoid growth from a hummock under the great cypress knees, surrounded by scum-green water that never felt sunlight, back in that Freudianly contorted cypress gloom of cottonmouth moccasins big as the biceps of a prize-fighter, and owl calls, and the murderous metallic grind of insect life, and the smudge fire at the hovel door, that door being nothing but a hole in the hovel wall, with a piece of croker sack hung over it. There were, a few miles off at the University, your colleagues, some as torpid as a gorged alligator in the cold mud of January and some avid to lick the spit of an indifferent or corrupt administration, but many able and gifted and fired by a will to create, out of the seething stew and heaving magma, a distinguished university.

And there were, of course, the students, like students anywhere in the country in the big state universities, except for the extraordinary number of pretty girls and the preternatural blankness of the gladiators who were housed beneath the stadium to have their reflexes honed, their diet supervised, and — through the efforts of tutors — their heads crammed with just enough of whatever mash was required (I never found out) to get them past their minimal examinations. Among the students there sometimes appeared, too, that awkward boy from the depth of the 'Cajun country or from some scrabble-farm in North Louisiana, with burning ambition and frightening energy and a thirst for learning; and his presence there, you reminded yourself, with whatever complication of irony seemed necessary at the moment, was due to Huey, and to Huey alone. For the "better element" had done next to nothing in fifty years to get that boy out of the grim despair of his ignorance.

Yes, there was the world of the "good families," most of whom hated Huey Long—except, of course, for that percentage who, for one reason or another, had reached an accommodation. They hated him sometimes for good reasons and sometimes for bad, and sometimes for no reason at all, as a mere revulsion of taste; but they never seemed to reflect on what I took to be the obvious fact that if the government of the state had not previously been marked by various combinations of sloth, complacency, incompetence, corruption, and a profound lack of political imagination, there would never have been a Senator Huey P. Long, and my old hitchhiker by the roadside would, in September 1934, have had no tale to tell me.

Conversation in Louisiana always came back to the tales, to the myth, to politics; and to talk politics is to talk about power. So conversation turned, by implication at least, on the question of power and ethics, of power and justification, of means and ends, of "historical costs." The big words were not often used, certainly not by the tellers of tales, but the concepts lurked even behind the most ungrammatical folktale. The tales were shot through with philosophy.

The tales were shot through, too, with folk humor, and the ethical ambiguity of folk humor. And the tales, like the political conversations, were shot through, too, with violence—or rather, with hints of the possibility of violence. There was a hint of revolutionary desperation—often synthetically induced. In Louisiana, in '34 and '35, it took nothing to start a rumor of violence. There had been, you might hear, a "battle" at the airport of Baton Rouge. A young filling station operator would proudly display his sawed-off automatic shotgun—I forget which "side" he was on, but I remember his fingers caressing the polished walnut of the stock. Or you might hear that there was going to be a "march" on the Capitol—but not by whom or for what.

Melodrama was the breath of life. There had been melodrama in the life I had known in Tennessee, but with a difference: in Tennessee the melodrama seemed to be different from the stuff of life, something superimposed upon life, but in Louisiana people lived melodrama, seemed to live, in fact, for it, for this strange combination of philosophy, humor, and violence. Life was a tale that you happened to be living—and that "Huey" happened to be living before your eyes. And all the while I was reading Elizabethan tragedy, Machiavelli, William James, and American history — and all that I was reading seemed to come alive, in shadowy distortions and sudden clarities, in what I saw around me.

How directly did I try to transpose into fiction Huey P. Long and the tone of that world? The question answers itself in a single fact. The first version of my story was a verse drama; and the actual writing began, in 1938, in the shade of an olive tree by a wheat field near Perugia. In other words, if you are sitting under an olive tree in Umbria and are writing a verse drama, the chances are that you are concerned more with the myth than with the fact, more with the symbolic than with the actual. And so it was. It could not, after all, have been otherwise, for in the strict, literal sense, I had no idea what the now deceased Huey P. Long had been. What I knew was the "Huey" of the myth, and that was what I had taken with me to Mussolini's Italy, where the bully boys wore black shirts and gave a funny salute.

I had no way of knowing what went on in the privacy of the heart of Senator Long. Now I could only hope, ambitiously, to know something of the heart of the Governor Talos of my play *Proud Flesh*. For Talos was the first avatar of my Willie Stark, and the fact that I drew that name from the "iron groom" who, in murderous blankness, serves Justice in Spenser's *Faerie Queen* should indicate something of the line of thought and feeling that led up to that version and persisted, with modulations into the novel.

Talos was to become Stark, and *Proud Flesh* was to become *All the King's Men*. Many things, some merely technical, led to this transformation, but one may have some bearing on the question of the ratio of fact and fiction. In 1942 I left Louisiana for good, and when in 1943 I began the version that is more realistic, discursive, and documentary in method (though not in spirit) than the play, I was doing so after I had definitely left Louisiana and the world in which the story had its roots. By now the literal, factual world was only a memory, and therefore was ready to be absorbed freely into the act of imagination. Even the old man by the roadside — the hitchhiker I had picked up on the way down to take my job — was ready to enter the story: he became, it would seem, the old hitch-hiker whom Jack Burden picks up returning from Long Beach, California, the old man with the twitch in the face that gives Jack the idea for the Great Twitch. But my old hitchhiker had had no twitch in his face. Nor had I been Jack Burden.

I had not been Jack Burden except in so far as you have to try to "be" whatever you are trying to create. And in that sense I was also Adam Stanton, and Willie Stark, and Sadie Burke, and Sugar Boy, and all the rest. And this brings me to my last notion. However important for my novel was the protracted dialectic between "Huey" on the one side, and me on the other, it was far less impor-tant, in the end, than that deeper and darker dialectic for which the images and actions of a novel are the only language. And however important was my acquaintance with Louisiana, that was far less important than my acquaintance with another country: for any novel, good or bad, must report, willy-nilly, the history, sociology, and politics of a country even more fantastic than was Louisiana under the consulship of Huey.

Arthur M. Schlesinger, Jr.

The Messiah of the Rednecks

... Thus ferment held out opportunity to those who could imprint their personalities on despair and offer distressed people an assur-

Reprinted from *The Politics of Upheaval* (Boston: Houghton Mifflin, 1960), pp. 42-68, by permission of the publisher. Copyright © 1960 by Arthur M. Schlesinger, Jr.

ance of the millennium. The question remained whether the unrest would shoot off in different directions under a multitude of leaders or whether one man could gather it all unto himself. For all their talents, neither Father Coughlin nor Dr. Townsend was in the tradition of major political achievement. If anyone could organize the discontent on a national basis and use it to propel himself into power, it would more probably be, not a priest nor a doctor, but a politician. The most likely candidate was surely the Senator from Louisiana, Huey Pierce Long, Jr.

II

Louisiana was as natural a breeding place for radicalism as its swamps were for fevers. No state in the Union had been so long misgoverned. The old oligarchy, a dreary alliance of New Orleans businessmen and upstate planters, controlled by the utilities, the railroads, and Standard Oil of Louisiana, had run things without serious challenge almost since Reconstruction. No state had so high a proportion of illiteracy: in 1928, when Huey Long was elected governor, probably one-fifth of the white men on the farms could not read or write. No state treated its children worse: in Louisiana, little boys and girls worked long hours in cane and strawberry fields, in mills and shrimp-packing plants. The system of roads was as run down as the system of schools. And the submerged people of Louisiana had not only been oppressed, they had been bored: no Cole Blease, no Tom Watson, no Heflin nor Bilbo had arisen to make them laugh and hate and to distract them from the drabness of their days. Half a century of pent-up redneck rancor was awaiting release.

Not all the state had acquiesced in the reign of the oligarchy. No part was more recalcitrant than the parish of Winn in the piny uplands of north central Louisiana, where poor white farmers worked the thin red soil for a meager living. During the Civil War, Winn had instructed its delegate to the state convention to vote against secession; it was derisively known as the Free State of Winn. When the Populist insurgency hit Louisiana, Winn was one of its centers. Twenty years later, it was a Socialist stronghold. In 1912, when Debs polled more votes in Louisiana than William Howard Taft, over a third of Winn Parish voted Socialist. The town of Winnfield, where Huey Long was born in 1893, elected an entire Socialist slate.

Young Huey's father, Huey Pierce Long, Sr., was a typical Winn Parish radical. "My father and my mother favored the Union. Why not? They didn't have slaves. They didn't even have decent land.

The rich folks had all the good land and all the slaves — why, their women didn't even comb their own hair. They'd sooner speak to a nigger than to a poor white." Life under the oligarchy had left unplumbed depths of resentment. "There wants to be a revolution, I tell you," old Huey said to a journalist in 1935. "I seen this domination of capital, seen it for seventy years. What do these rich folks care for the poor man? They are nothing — not for his pain, his sickness, nor his death. . . . Maybe you're surprised to hear me talk like that. Well, it was just such talk that my boy was raised under."

Young Huey was the seventh of nine children. He was born in a log house, but it was a comfortable four-room unit, and he was not reared in poverty. Still, he could not escape the drudgery of country life. "From my earliest recollection," he later said, "I hated the farm work. . . . Rising before the sun, we toiled until dark, after which we did nothing except eat supper, listen to the whippoorwills, and go to bed." Only politics and religion — both highly revivalist in style — relieved the tedium. A bright, rather bookish lad, Huey was resolved to be anything but a farmer. He read avidly, particularly romantic history and fiction — J. C. Ridpath's florid *History of the World*, and Scott, Dumas, and Victor Hugo. He attended church, became a champion debater in high school, and spent his free time in the local printing office. He was not a tough boy. His younger brother Earl used to say in later years, "I had to do all of Huey's fighting for him."

In 1910, when Huey was seventeen, his debating talent won him a scholarship to Louisiana State University. But he lacked money for books and living expenses; so he put his volubility to other uses and became a traveling salesman. He sold furniture, soap, groceries, patent medicines for "women's sickness" and a vegetable shortening product called Cottolene. As part of his Cottolene pitch, he organized cooking contests; the winner in Shreveport was a pretty girl named Rose McConnell, with whom he fell in love — or at least so the story went, as certified by all except Huey in his autobiography. In 1912, having strayed as far west as Oklahoma, Long spent a few months at the University of Oklahoma Law School, "the happiest days of my life." When the session ended, he returned to the road. In 1913 he married Rose McConnell, and the next year, with a few hundred dollars of savings and a loan from his brother Julius, he entered Tulane Law School in New Orleans. Now he applied himself with frenzied determination. Studying from sixteen to twenty hours a day, he completed a three-year law course in eight months. Then he talked the Chief Justice of the state into giving him a special bar

examination. In May 1915 he was sworn in as a lawyer. He was
twenty-one years old.[1]

III

The young man made an office out of the small anteroom over the
bank in Winnfield. He put his three law books on a white pine-top
table, and a fifty-cent tin sign announced "HUEY P. LONG, LAWYER."
The shoe store next door agreed to take his phone calls. Business was slow to come. He was ambitious and sensitive. When he
appeared before a legislative committee to plead for a better work-
men's-compensation law, he was kidded and laughed at by the
senators; this gave him a dislike of legislatures. He failed to receive
an expected appointment as Assistant United States Attorney; this,
too, wounded him. "Once disappointed over a political undertaking,
I could never cast it from my mind. I awaited the opportunity of a
political contest."

In the meantime, the United States entered the First World War.
"I did not go," Long later said, "because I was not mad at anybody
over there." A notary public, he claimed draft exemption as a state
official. When State Senator S. J. Harper, an old Winnfield radical,
was indicted by a federal grand jury for writing a book warning
that profiteers would take advantage of the war to establish financial slavery, Long was his lawyer and secured his acquittal. It was
under Harper's influence that Long published a letter in the *New
Orleans Item* on March 1, 1918, under the headline "THINKS
WEALTH SHOULD BE MORE EVENLY DISTRIBUTED." In it Long ar-
gued that 2 per cent of the people owned 70 per cent of the wealth,
that the rich were growing richer and the poor poorer, and that
inequality of educational opportunity was widening the gap between
classes. "With wealth concentrating, classes becoming defined," he
concluded, "there is not the opportunity for Christian uplift and
education and cannot be until there is more economic reform. That
is the problem that the good people of this country must consider."

---

[1] Huey P. Long, *Every Man A King* (New Orleans, 1933), Chs. 1-2; V.O.
Key, Jr., *Southern Politics in State and Nation* (New York, 1949), 151-61;
Grady McWhiney, "Louisiana Socialists in the Early Twentieth Century,"
Journal of Southern History, Aug. 1954; James Rorty, "Callie Long's Boy
Huey," *Forum*, Aug. 1935; Forrest Davis, *Huey Long, A Candid Biography*
(New York, 1935), Chs. 3-4; Carlton Beals, *The Story of Huey Long* (Phila-
delphia, 1935), Ch. 2; H. F. Kane, *Louisiana Hayride* (New York, 1941),
Ch. 2; H. B. Deutsch, "Prelude to a Heterocrat," *Saturday Evening Post*,
Sept. 7, 1935.

And Huey Long meant to help the good people in their considera-
tion. After a careful examination of the state constitution, he found
that the post of Railroad Commissioner had no prescribed age limit.
In 1918, twenty-five years old, he announced for this office, noisily
assailed the big corporations, and won election. During the next
nine years on the Railroad Commission and its successor, the Public
Service Commission, Huey seized every opportunity to dramatize
himself as the champion of the people against the oil companies,
the telephone company, the utilities, and the railroads. Nor was
this all merely whooping and hollering. His shrewd and persistent
attacks put the companies on the defensive and brought rates down.

In 1924 he tried to cash in on this record by running for governor.
It was too soon; he was barely thirty-one years old. And he was
caught in the cross fire between the Klan and its opponents. Long
straddled this issue; despite his poor white sympathies, he did not,
like Hugo Black in Alabama, join the Klan.

A few months before the 1928 primaries he again showed up as
a candidate, his followers parading under a banner reading (the
phrase was adapted from William Jennings Bryan): "EVERY MAN A
KING, BUT NO ONE WEARS A CROWN." Huey campaigned furiously
around the state, speaking at dusty crossroads and in shaded courthouse squares, his voice raucous and confiding, his arms pumping
up and down, his seersucker suit stained with sweat. The poor white
farmers — lean, leather-faced, rawboned men, surly and proud —
crowded to see him. When he deluged the prominent figures in the
community with unsparing personal abuse, they shouted, "Pour it
on 'em, Huey! Pour it on 'em!" The oligarchy bewailed his uncouth-
ness, his vituperation, his lack of dignity. "This State's full of sap-
sucker, hillbilly, and Cajun relations of mine," Long replied, "and
there ain't enough dignity in the bunch to keep a chigger still long
enough to go brush his hair." And the sapsuckers, the hillbillys, and
the Cajuns, the woolhats and the rednecks, laughed and cheered
and voted for one of their own. In 1928 they elected Huey Long
Governor of Louisiana. He was now thirty-five.

IV

Thus far it was a familiar southern pattern—the ambitious young
politician from the sticks, making his way to the top by rousing the
boobs and denouncing the interests. The next step seemed obvious
enough; now he would exact his price for peace with the people he
had so long assailed. After all, Huey Long was no model of pecuniary

virtue. He himself admitted that in the twenties legal fees from large corporations enabled him to build "a modern home in the best residential section of the City of Shreveport at a cost of $40,000." His brother Julius told a Senate committee that Huey's 1924 gubernatorial campaign was largely financed by the Southwestern Gas and Electric Company. Earl Long said that Huey took a $10,000 bribe from a utility executive in 1927. (Huey cried, "That is a God damn lie.") If the interests would pay the price, they could presumably take Long into the same camp they had taken so many others.

And so the merchants and the respectable politicians of New Orleans tendered the Governor-elect an elaborate banquet. But they underestimated their man. Though Huey would occasionally sell for a price, he could never be relied on to deliver. His essential ambition was not money but power, and he did not want to share the power with anybody else. He proposed now to smash the oligarchy and gain undisputed power for himself. Nor, perhaps, was it just for himself. Huey had not forgotten the poor people of *Louisiana*. As Governor, he was determined to increase school appropriations, to provide free textbooks, to pave highways and bridge rivers, to build charity hospitals and insane asylums. Long knew where the money was coming from—the big corporations, and especially Standard Oil.

He launched his program with characteristic vigor. When the legislature balked, the Governor appeared personally at the Capitol to cajole, threaten, browbeat, and bribe. He ignored the separation of powers, treated senators and representatives with unconcealed contempt, and bulled through enactments with careless confidence. One opponent shoved a volume before the Governor: "Maybe you've heard of this book. It's the Constitution of the State of Louisiana." "I'm the Constitution around here now," Long replied.

In 1929, when Long called a special session of the legislature to place an occupational tax of five cents a barrel on refined crude oil, his enemies decided that the time had come. Standard Oil and other corporations feared the tax as a fatal precedent. Constitutionalists thought that Huey Long's technique of personal government was threatening democracy. The oligarchy saw its power crumbling away before the pile-driver onslaughts of a redneck revolutionist. If they could not buy Long, they would break him. Their response was to demand his impeachment. A scatter-gun indictment accused the Governor of virtually every impeachable act except (oddly) drunkenness; he was even charged with plotting the assassination of an opposition representative. For a moment, Long was on the defensive. But he fought back savagely, haranguing audiences around the state and bringing incessant pressure on members of the Senate. Finally

enough senators signed a round robin citing technical objections to
the indictment to deny the opposition the necessary two-thirds.
Huey was in the clear. The experience only deepened his resentment. He said later, "I used to try to get things done by saying
'please.' That didn't work and now I'm a dynamiter. I dynamite 'em
out of my path."

In the next months, as his brother Julius said, "He politicalized
everything in the State that could be politicalized." Julius added,
"He holds every State office; every State office," and "There has
never been such an administration of ego and pomposity since the
days of Nero." Huey was now more shameless than ever in crushing
out opposition. "They beat a man almost to death, if he does not
agree with them," said Julius Long, "and not a thing is done about
it. The people that were supposed to enforce the laws in this State
have become a howling, lawless mob. . . . A human life is not safe,
and neither is his property." "I did not know how they hold elec-
tions in Mexico or Russia or anywhere else," said Earl Long, "but
I do not think they could surpass what has been going on in
Louisiana."

Dynamiting everything out of his path, Huey moved to complete
the humiliation of the oligarchy. In 1930 he announced his candi-
dacy for the Senate to succeed J. E. Ransdell, the respectable conservative who had been senator since 1913. At the same time, he
made it clear that he would not resign as Governor until he had
served out his term lest the anti-Long Lieutenant Governor sabo-
tage his program. And he described the election itself as a referen-
dum on his policies. After a turbulent campaign, climaxed by the
kidnaping of two men who threatened to expose corruption in the
administration, Long carried the day. The country boy from the
red slopes and loblolly pines of Winn Parish was now on the national
stage.[2]

V

In his manners, values, and idiom, Huey Long remained a back-
country hillbilly. But he was a hillbilly raised to the highest level,
preternaturally swift and sharp in intelligence, ruthless in action,

---

[2] Long, *Every Man A King*, Chs. 3-12, 15-16; Davis, *Long*, Chs. 4, 6; Beals,
Long, Chs. 3-16; Walter Davenport, "Yes, Your Excellency," *Collier's*, Dec.
13, 1930; A. M. Shaw, "The First Time I saw Huey," *Southwest Review*,
Winter, 1950; Senate Committee on Investigation of Campaign Expenditures,
Senatorial Campaign Expenditures, 1932 (*Louisiana*); *Hearings*, 72 Cong.,
2 Sess. (1933), 817, 822, 841, 953, 957, 964-67; *Congressional Record*, 73 Cong.,
1 Sess. (March 13, 1933), 275.

and grandiose in vision. He was a man of medium height, well-built but inclining toward pudginess. His dress was natty and loud. His face was round, red, and blotched, with more than a hint of pouches and jowls. Its rubbery mobility, along with the curly red-brown hair and the oversize putty nose, gave him the deceptive appearance of a clown. But the darting popeyes could easily turn from soft to hard, and the cleft chin was strong and forceful. At times it was a child's face, spoiled and willful; he looked, noted John Dos Passos, "like an overgrown small boy with very bad habits indeed." At times, it was the face of the cunning yokel about to turn the tables on the city slickers around him. At times, it became exceedingly hard and cruel.

In relaxation, Long had the lethargic air of an upcountry farmer. He liked to slump drowsily on a chair or stretch out on a sofa or loll on a bed. In certain moods, he would talk quietly, grammatically, and sensibly, with humor and perception. But he was always likely to explode into violent activity, leaping to his feet, hunching his shoulders, waving his arms, roaring with laughter or rage, emphasizing points by pounding furniture or clapping people on the back. "The phone rang every minute or so while we talked," said James Thurber, "and he would get up and walk through a couple of rooms to answer it and come back and fling himself heavily on the bed again so that his shoulders and feet hit it at the same moment." The jerkiness of his movements reminded one observer of the flickering figures rushing across the screen in early silent films. This very intensity underlined his coarse and feverish power.

His weakness for conducting business in bed won him his first national notoriety. On a Sunday morning in March 1930, while Huey was recovering from the diversions of the night before in his suite at the Hotel Roosevelt in New Orleans, the commander of the German cruiser *Emden*, in dress uniform, accompanied by the German consul in morning coat, paid a courtesy call on the Governor of Louisiana. Hearing that guests were outside, Huey flung a red and blue dressing gown over green silk pajamas, shuffled on blue bedroom slippers, and ambled affably into the next room. His visitors left somewhat stiffly. Soon after, the German consul complained that Long had insulted the German Reich by his attire and demanded an apology. Long, somewhat amused, explained that he was just a boy from the country. "I know little of diplomacy and much less of the international courtesies and exchanges that are indulged in by nations." The next day, having collected all the elements of formal morning dress except a top hat, the Governor, in

tail coat but with a snappy gray fedora, boarded the *Emden* and
made his apologies.

The incident delighted the press across the nation, and Huey
became for the first time a front-page figure outside Louisiana. It
may also have given him some ideas. For the first time he was
receiving friendly notices. All the world loved a character; might
it not be that the disguise of comedy could make people overlook
or forgive much else? He had always been a jocose figure, given to
ribald language and homely anecdotes. From this time forward he
began to cultivate a public reputation as a buffoon. And the new
public persona happily acquired a name. In the ribbing which took
place around the Executive Mansion, Huey took to calling one of
his gang "Brother Crawford," after a character in the Amos 'n Andy
radio program; in return he was called "Kingfish," after the head
of Amos and Andy's lodge, the Mystic Knights of the Sea. Once
someone questioned his right to be present at a meeting of the
Highway Commission. "I looked around at the little fishes present,"
Long explained later, "and said, 'I'm the Kingfish.' " The title stuck.
Huey himself used to claim that the name "Long" was hard to get
over the telephone, so that it saved time to say, "This is the Kingfish." Also, he added, it substituted "gaiety for some of the tragedy
of politics." In the same vein, he started a mock debate over whether
cornpone should be crumbled or dunked in potlikker — the liquid
left at the bottom of the pot after boiling vegetable greens and pork
fat. This became a national issue. Even Franklin D. Roosevelt,
Governor of New York but a Georgian by adoption, joined the argument. Roosevelt was a crumbler. Long, a dunker, finally agreed to
a compromise.

But all the Kingfish's clowning could not conceal his more formidable qualities, especially his power and speed of mind. His intelligence, Raymond Moley once said, was an instrument such as is
given to few men. As Governor, he was an efficient administrator,
sure in detail, quick in decision. On his legal mettle, before a court-
room or arguing the case for seating his Louisiana delegation at the
Democratic convention of 1932, he displayed a disciplined and razor-
keen analytical ability. Still, he did not value his gift. As Moley
said, "He misused it, squandered it, battered it, as a child might
treat a toy. . . . He used his mind so erratically as to seem, a great
deal of the time, not only childish but insane." Alben Barkley once
told him, "You are the smartest lunatic I ever saw in my whole
life!" (Long rejoined, "Maybe that is the smartest description I've
ever had applied to me!")

He was not a nice man. When his brother Julius asked him in 1930 to give their aged father a room in the Executive Mansion, Huey complained bitterly about "base ingratitude and threatened holdups" and refused. "I swear," Julius said later, "that I do not know of a man, any human being, that has less feelings for his family than Huey P. Long has." The yes men and hoodlums who clustered around him were bound to him by fear or by greed, not by affection. He knew he was much smarter than anyone else, and he could not conceal his contempt for others. He told legislators to their faces that he could buy and sell them "like sacks of potatoes." He called officeholders "dime-a-dozen punks." He rejoiced in deeds of personal humiliation. Revenge was always prominent in his mind. His flippant brutality was both evidence of his mastery and a further source of his power.

On the hustings, he played on his listeners with intimate knowledge, deriding them, insulting them, whipping up emotions of resentment and spite, contemptuously providing them with scapegoats. He knew what to say to produce the response he wanted, and, knowing, said it. "If he went in a race up North," Julius Long said, "he would publish up there that there is part nigger in us in order to get the nigger vote."

Vilification was his particular weapon. His blistering frontier invective provided the link between his own superior intelligence and the surging envy of the crowds before him. He expressed what his hearers had long felt but could not say. He was their idol — themselves as they would like to be, free and articulate and apparently without fear. It was only when he had left the platform, when hard-faced bodyguards closed in around him, shoving his admirers back and moving in a flying wedge toward the black limousine, it was only then that it became evident that Huey Long was a coward — the "yellowest physical coward," his brother Earl said, "that God had ever let live."

He carried these qualities to Washington — the comic impudence, the gay egotism, the bravado, the mean hatred, the fear. He was a man propelled by a greed for power and a delight in its careless exercise. "The only sincerity there was in him," said Julius Long, "was for himself." He talked broadly about the need for redistributing the wealth, but these were words. When a reporter tried to discover deeper meanings, Long brushed him off: "I haven't any program or any philosophy. I just take things as they come." Yet, for all this, there remained the sense in which his qualities and his ambitions were those of the plain people of his state writ large — the people from the red clay country and the piny woods, from the canebrakes and the bayous, the shrimp fishermen and the moss fishermen, the rednecks and the hillbillies and the Cajuns. Once, standing before the Evangeline Oak, he spoke to the Acadians of southern Louisiana and recalled the legend of Evangeline, weeping for her vanished lover. She was not, Long said, the only Acadian thus to have waited and wept.

> Where are the schools that you have waited for your children to have, that have never come? Where are the roads and the highways that you spent your money to build, that are no nearer now than ever before? Where are the institutions to care for the sick and disabled? Evangeline wept bitter tears in her disappointment. But they lasted only one lifetime. Your tears . . . have lasted for generations.

His conclusion seemed to come from the heart: "Give me the chance to dry the tears of those who still weep here."

His strength, observed Sherwood Anderson, lay in "the terrible South that Stark Young and his sort ignore . . . the beaten, ignorant, Bible-ridden, white South. Faulkner occasionally really touches it. It has yet to be paid for." That terrible South was exacting the price of years of oppression. Huey Long was its man, and he gave it by proxy the delights it had been so long denied.[3] . . .

XII

At the beginning of 1935, in his forty-second year, Long gave off a sense of destiny. Would there be a third party in 1936? "Sure to be. And I think we will sweep the country." Foreign visitors found him impressive, though unattractive. Rebecca West detected the steely intelligence behind the Mardi Gras mask of his conversation:

[3] Davenport, "Yes, Your Excellency"; Walter Davenport, "How Huey Long Gets Away With It," *Collier's*, June 17, 1933; Davenport, "The Robes of the Kingfish," *Collier's*, Nov. 22, 1935; Sen. Com. on Investigation of Campaign Expenditures, *Senatorial Campaign Expenditures*, 954-56, 963; John Dos Passos, "Washington: The Big Tent," *New Republic*, March 14, 1934; "Talk of the Town," *New Yorker*, Sept. 2, 1933; Jerome Beatty, "You Can't Laugh Him Off," *American*, Jan. 1933; Mildred Adams, "Huey the Great," *Forum*, Feb. 1933; Russell Owen, "Huey Long Keeps Washington Guessing," *New York Times Magazine*, Jan. 29, 1933; Owen, "Huey Long Gives His Views of Dictators," *New York Times Magazine*, Feb. 10, 1935; M. O. Frost, "Huey Long 'Purifies' Louisiana," *Today*, Aug. 3, 1934; Hamilton Basso, "Huey Long and His Background," *Harper's*, May 1935; Raymond Moley, *27 Masters of Politics* (New York, 1949), 221; Alben Barkley, *That Reminds Me* (New York, 1954), 159; *New York Times*, Oct. 18, 1932; Long, *Every Man A King*, especially Chs. 14, 27; Davis, *Long*, especially Chs. 5-6; H. T. Kane, "Louisiana Story," *New York Times Magazine*, Sept. 27, 1959; Sherwood Anderson, *Letters*, H. M. Jones, ed. (Boston, 1953, 310-11.

"He is the most formidable kind of brer fox, the self-abnegating kind that will profess ignorance, who will check his dignity with his hat if he can serve his plans by buffoonery." She said later, "In his vitality and his repulsiveness he was very like Laval." He reminded H. G. Wells of "a Winston Churchill who has never been at Harrow."

Yet the nature of this destiny remained obscure, even to him. All he had was a sense of crisis and of opportunity. Once during the Hundred Days he had said to a group in the Senate cloakroom, "Men, it will not be long until there will be a mob assembling here to hang Senators from the rafters of the Senate. I have to determine whether I will stay and be hung with you, or go out and lead the mob." ("That statement," Senator Richard B. Russell reported later, "evoked very little laughter.") Was he a demagogue? "There are all kinds of demagogues," he said. "Some deceive the people in the interests of the lords and masters of creation, the Rockefellers and the Morgans. Some of them deceive the people in their own interest." He often said, with his impish grin, "What this country needs is a dictator." But he also said, "I don't believe in dictatorships, all these Hitlers and Mussolinis. They don't belong in our American life. And Roosevelt is a bigger dictator than any." Then again: "There is no dictatorship in Louisiana. There is a perfect democracy there, and when you have a perfect democracy it is pretty hard to tell it from a dictatorship.". He told a gullible interviewer from the *New Republic*, "It's all in Plato. You know — the Greek philosopher. I hadn't read Plato before I wrote my material on the 'Share the Wealth' movement, and when I did read Plato afterwards, I found I had said almost exactly the same things. I felt as if I had written Plato's *Republic* myself."

In 1935 some people wondered whether Long was the first serious American fascist. Long himself, when George Sokolsky asked him about it, laughed it off: "Fine. I'm Mussolini and Hitler rolled in one. Mussolini gave them caster oil; I'll give them tabasco, and then they'll like Louisiana." But he was no Hitler or Mussolini. He had no ideological preoccupations; he never said, "When the United States gets fascism it will call it anti-fascism," nor was he likely to think in such terms. Read *Mein Kampf*, and one sees a man possessed by a demonic dream which he must follow until he can purge all evil from the world. Read *Every Man A King*, and one finds a folksy and rather conventional chronicle of political success. Read Long's *My First Days in the White House*, ghost-written by a Hearst reporter in 1935, and one has a complacent picture of a painless triumph, with Rockefeller, Mellon and the du Ponts backing

President Long in his project of sharing the wealth (the book did have one engaging impudence: in choosing his cabinet, Long appointed as his Secretary of the Navy Franklin D. Roosevelt). Long's political fantasies had no tensions, no conflicts, except of the most banal kind, no heroism or sacrifice, no compelling myths of class or race or nation.

He had no overriding social vision. According to Raymond Daniell, who covered him for the *New York Times*, he did believe in Share Our Wealth "with all his heart"; but it was as a technique of political self-aggrandizement, not as a gospel of social reconstruction. Part traveling salesman, part confidence man, part gang leader, he had at most a crude will toward personal power. He had no doubt about becoming President: the only question was whether it was to be in 1936 or 1940. He told Forrest Davis that he planned to destroy both major parties, organize a single party of his own, and serve four terms. To Daniell he disclosed "the whole scheme by which he hoped to establish himself as the dictator of this country." His hero was Frederick the Great, and he no doubt saw himself as a kind of Frederick the Great from the piney woods. ("He was the greatest son of a bitch who ever lived. 'You can't take Vienna, Your Majesty. The world won't stand for it,' his nitwit ambassadors said. 'The hell I can't,' said old Fred, 'my soldiers will take Vienna and my professors at Heidelberg will explain the reasons why!' Hell, I've got a university down in Louisiana that cost me $15,000,000 that can tell you why I do like I do.")

At bottom, Huey Long resembled, not a Hitler or a Mussolini, but a Latin American dictator, a Vargas or a Perón. Louisiana was in many respects a colonial region, an underdeveloped area; its Creole traditions gave it an almost Latin American character. Like Vargas and Perón, Long was in revolt against economic colonialism, against the oligarchy, against the smug and antiquated past; like them, he stood in a muddled way for economic modernization and social justice; like them, he was most threatened by his own arrogance and cupidity, his weakness for soft living and his rage for personal power.

And, like them, he could never stop. "I was born into politics," he once said, "a wedded man, with a storm for my bride." A man of violence, he generated an atmosphere of violence. Early in 1935 Mason Spencer, one of Long's last foes still on his feet in the Louisiana legislature, sent the Kingfish a solemn warning.

"I am not gifted with second sight," Spencer said. "Nor did I see a spot of blood on the moon last night.

"But I can see blood on the polished floor of this Capitol.

"For if you ride this thing through, you will travel with the white
horse of death." [4]

[4] H. G. Wells, *The New America: The New World* (New York, 1935), 29;
Rebecca West, "The Kaleidoscope That Is Washington," *New Republic*, May
12, 1935; Rebecca West to author, Jan. 20, 1959; *Congressional Record*, 84
Cong., 1 Sess. 3637 (April 13, 1955); Owen, "Long Keeps Washington Gues-
sing"; Russell Owen, "Huey Long Gives His Views of Dictators," *New York
Times Magazine*, Feb. 10, 1935; *New York Times*, March 26, 1933; Rose Lee,
"Senator Long At Home," *New Republic*, May 30, 1934; George Sokolsky,
"Huey Long," *Atlantic*, Nov. 1935; Huey P. Long, *My First Days in the White
House* (Harrisburg, 1935); F. Raymond Daniell, "Land of the Free," in Han-
son Baldwin and Shepard Stone, eds., *We Saw It Happen* (New York, 1938),
90-91; Davis, *Long*, 22, 41, 204, 287; *Time*, April 1, 1935; Carter, "Huey Long,"
343; B. L. Hoteling, "Long as a Journalist," *Journalism Quarterly*, March
1943; Williams, "Gentleman from Louisiana."

Robert Penn Warren

Knowledge And The Image of Man

Our general topic is Man's Right to Knowledge. To put my cart
before the horse, the conclusion before the discussion, and let the cat
out of the bag, I'll assert that to say man's right to knowledge is
simply a way of saying man's right to exist, to be himself, to be
a man.

That, of course, is the premise of our society — man's right to
exist as a man, as a uniquely defined individual. Our society, we
know well, violates this premise every day, but it remains fundamental to our democratic Western world.

We must distinguish this idea from the idea of the sanctity of life
as such. More frequently in other societies than ours has the saint or
sage turned from the caterpillar in the path or shrunk to pluck the
lettuce for fear of the unhearable scream. No, we have limited and
revised the idea of the sanctity of life. Human life we mean in our
world, and human life not as existence but as the individual's right

Reprinted from *Sewanee Review*, LXIII (Spring, 1955), 182-92, by permission
of the William Morris Agency. Copyright © 1955 by the University of the
South.

to exist as himself, the right to the hazards and glories of trying to develop most fully as himself.

I suppose that this notion of personality — the right to define oneself — despite all the distortions it has suffered from forces like Machiavellianism, Manchester economics, the Winning of the West, and progressive education, is a heritage of Christianity. Every soul is valuable in God's sight, and the story of every soul is the story of its self-definition for good or evil, salvation or damnation. Every soul is valuable in God's sight. Or, with the secularization of things, we may say: every soul is valuable in man's sight.

If we accept this notion, then we are committed to recognize the right of every soul to that knowledge necessary for its best fulfillment.

At this point, however, someone may object to the statement that man's right to knowledge, in our society at least, derives from, or is related to, our Christian history. The objector may recollect that every Christian church has, at one time or another, opposed the extension of knowledge. To this objection one may say that the various churches are of this world and have made their worldly errors, and that opposition to the extension of knowledge, in any given instance, was accidental and not essential to Christianity; and one could paraphrase Jacques Maritain in another context: the glory of God does not demand that man go on all fours.

To be a man, to keep from going on all fours, implies the right to knowledge. But it is a sad fact that, though the glory of God does not demand that man go on all fours the glory of our democracy, by a last perversion, sometimes seems to make that demand. Since I am about to refer to the Age of the Common Man, I shall hasten to say that I was a New Dealer, with as few reservations and heart burnings as one can reasonably expect about a political process, and I don't take it back now. But one of the heart burnings I did have was precisely about Common Man-ism of the sort the New Deal *sometimes* promoted.

The prophets of the Common Man might have spoken gloriously — if they had really believed that that fellow-citizen whom they called the Common Man was really as good as they, the prophets, too often took themselves to be. But no, they often spoke with a nauseous condescension, and it was not glorious. They might have said something like this: As men we have in common certain capacities that make us men, the capacity to envisage ourselves in relation to nature and other men, the capacity for self-criticism, the capacity for a disinterested love of excellence. Let us try, therefore, to create a society in which each man may develop as far as possible those capacities that distinguish his manhood, and in which each man will accept his responsibility for trying to realize his common humanity at its highest.

Perhaps some of the prophets did speak gloriously, but their voices were generally drowned out by voices that in declaring the Age of the Common Man uttered a doctrine of complacency. These voices, by implication at least, denied that democracy should mean the opportunity — and the responsibility — for the development of excellence, and uttered a doctrine carrying at its core the appalling convictions that the undeveloped, the unaspiring, the frustrated, the un-responsible, is somehow mystically superior to the excellent, and that a refusal of effort toward excellence is a gesture of moral worth.

In reading the history of our country we have met all too often this same old notion, the glorification of the un-excellent, this conviction that a mystic worth attaches to ignorance. Sometimes this was, we know, a way of pitting the honest coon-skin cap against crowns and coronets, an honest faith in democracy against Norman blood. But looking back on our forefathers, we know, too, that they were not above the human frailty of an awkward and strident defensiveness in the face of the learning, grace, and achievement of the Old World, and that, to keep their courage up, they whistled a little in the dark of their own heads.

Looking back, we can applaud the sturdy independence, the faith in democracy and destiny, and the lethal efficiency of the long-rifle levelled at a Redcoat. We can relish the juicy rambunctiousness and wild poetry and courage of the frontier, and see the pathos of its loneliness, malaria, and degradation. But this does not mean that, in the end, we have to take Davy Crockett as a philosopher superior to Immanuel Kant.

This isn't quite what happened in 1933, but it is uncomfortably close. And part of the sad comedy was that one of the places where the process flourished most rankly was in some classrooms of literature, especially of American literature, and in learned books on that subject. To study our culture sometimes meant to seek out documentations of Common Man-ism. I am not referring merely to those students of our culture who made a Holy Alliance with Stalin and interpreted our history as a blundering and uninstructed provincial attempt to be Russian. No, I am referring to that far greater number who were devoted to the American Dream and the American Mission, but whose devotion manifested itself as an easy and sometimes false documentation of Common Man-ism, a process that took the place of the investigation of all other values, and I do not mean what it was sometimes fashionable to refer to as "merely literary values." I mean all values, including those of common sense and simple honesty.

Whitman was split down the middle and the part of his work that is humanly full was rejected for what was politically viable. Flaubert had nothing to tell us in an age of crisis. Down with Hardy and up with Ruth Suckow and Rölvaag or Grace Lumpkin. "Snowbound" is a great poem, and Henry James betrayed America. Conrad is not socially relevant, for he merely treats of man against geography. Faulkner is a Gothic fascist, and hates Negroes.

Most of the people who adopted these views were simply innocent, with decent human sympathies, but their very virtues made it possible in that context to accept the fashionable thing, and the fashionable thing simply amounted to the notion that only the easy and immediate is valuable. The Spirit of God may not be in you, but the spirit of Democracy sure is, and if you are a Common Man, all things shall be added unto you, without your turning a hand, and anyway you've probably already got everything worth having. So the Right to Knowledge, which should have meant the glorification of our common human capacity to move toward excellence, to define ourselves in a communal aspiration, was betrayed by the prophets of Common Man-ism.

Not only was the Right to Knowledge betrayed. There was an even more gross betrayal. The complacency fostered by the doctrine of Common Man-ism belied and betrayed that aspiration to excellence that is really in our midst, that has always marked much of our history, an aspiration that is sometimes blundering and confused but is indomitable and indestructible. It must be indestructible, more indestructible even than the cat in the adage, for it has survived even the attempt of the New Deal to choke it with butter.

All this has been, in a way, an aside, the self-indulgent venting of old spleen, but too, I trust, a description of one extreme threat to the Right to Knowledge — the threat from well-meaning friends. We have less to fear sometimes from the Powers of Darkness than from would-be Angels of Light, and the would-be Angels of Light change their plumage from time to time. Right now the fashionable cut in wings and haloes is not that of the New Deal.

Let us come back to our beginning, the statement that the right to exist as a man assumes the Right to Knowledge.

It assumes the right because only by knowledge does man achieve his identity. I do not mean that the mere implements of knowledge — books, libraries, laboratories, seminars — distinguish man from the brute. No, knowledge gives him his identity because it gives him the image of himself. And the image of himself necessarily has a foreground and a background, for man is in the world not as a billiard ball placed on a table, not even as a ship on the ocean with location determinable by latitude and longitude. He is, rather, in the world with continual and intimate interpenetration, an inevitable osmosis of being, which in the end does not deny, but affirms, his identity. It affirms it, for out of a progessive understanding of this interpenetration, this texture of relations, man creates new perspectives, discovers new values — that is, a new self — and so the identity is a continually emerging, an unfolding, a self-affirming and, we hope, a self-corrective creation.

Despite this osmosis of being to which I have referred, man's process of self-definition means that he distinguishes himself from the world and from other men. He disintegrates his primal instinctive sense of unity, he discovers separateness. In this process he discovers the pain of self-criticism and the pain of isolation. But the pain may, if he is fortunate, develop its own worth, work its own homeopathic cure. In the pain of self-criticism he may develop an ideal of excellence, and an ideal of excellence, once established, implies a de-personalized communion in that ideal. In the pain of isolation he may achieve the courage and clarity of mind to envisage the tragic pathos of life, and once he realizes that the tragic experience is universal and a corollary of man's place in nature, he may return to a communion with man and nature.

Man can return to his lost unity, and if that return is fitful and precarious, if the foliage and flower of the innocent garden are now somewhat browned by a late season, all is the more precious for the fact, for what is now achieved has been achieved by a growth of moral awareness. The return to nature and man is the discovery of love, and law. But love through separateness, and law through rebellion. Man eats of the fruit of the Tree of Knowledge, and falls. But if he takes another bite, he may get at least a sort of redemption. And a precious redemption. His unity with nature will not now be that of a drop of water in the ocean; it is, rather, the unity of the lover with the beloved, a unity presupposing separateness. His unity with mankind will not now be the unity of a member of the tribal horde with that pullulating mass; his unity will be that of a member of sweet society.

I suppose that the ultimate unity of knowledge is in the image of himself that man creates through knowledge, the image of his destiny, the mask he stares at. This would mean that manipulative knowledge, as well as knowledge of vision, calculation as well as conception—to take Shelley's distinction—works toward the creation of that image. Or to take another set of distinctions, the knowledge of *make*, that of *do*, that of *see*, that of *be*, however sharply we may distinguish them for various purposes, ultimately interfuse in our life process. Any change of environment — including any making — creates a new relation between man and his world, and other men. Any doing changes the doer. Any seeing changes the see-er. And any knowledge one has of his own being modifies that being, re-creates it, and thus changes the quality of making, doing, seeing.

Here let us remind ourselves most emphatically that a change in man's image of himself is not necessarily for the better. We do not ride a gravy train. We have seen, and see, in our own time, certain self-images of Frankensteinian horror that have captured the imagination of whole peoples. So new knowledge may give us new images absurd or dangerous, or may inadequately revise an old image so that it becomes absurd or dangerous, an anachronism. An intimate knowledge of fruit flies may lead us to think of human needs and values at the level of the fruit fly. A knowledge of the domestic arrangements of ancient royal houses of Egypt, or of Shelley's idea that incest is the most poetic of subjects, may lead us to a new admiration for the goings-on of the Jukeses and Kallikaks. And a knowledge of the structure of the atom may lead us to destroy ourselves. I say that knowledge *may* lead us to such unfortunate conclusions. But need it? And if it does, must we blame knowledge? No, we should blame incompleteness of knowledge — the fact that knowledge of human nature, human needs, human values, has not kept pace with knowledge of fruit flies and atoms, the fact that we have not achieved balance and responsibility in the ever-unfolding process of self-definition.

When we ourselves must combat the force of some absurd or dangerous image of man — the image of man, say, that stood behind Nazism — we run the risk of assimilating the horror in the very act of wrestling with it. We run that risk because such an image, horrible though it may be, could not exist at all, or compel the imagination of millions, if it did not spring from, and satisfy, certain human needs, and give scope for certain human virtues. By our own similar needs and similar virtues we are vulnerable to the temptation of that image. As Coleridge says, all beliefs are true; at least, the fact of their existence proves that there is a kind of truth in them. To say this is not to condone a horror, but to realize its fullness in the fact that its energies of evil are a perversion of energies potential for good, that the will for destruction is but the will for creation swayed from its proper end.

And I am reminded here of the profound passage in Conrad's *Lord Jim*, when Marlow comments on the apparently aimless massaacre by the brigand Brown:

Thus Brown balanced his account with the evil fortune. Notice that even in this awful outbreak there is a superiority as of a man who carries right — the abstract thing — within the envelope of his common desires. It was not a vulgar and treacherous massacre; it was a lesson, a retribution—a demonstration of some obscure and awful attribute of our nature which, I am afraid, is not so very far under the surface as we like to think.

Even in the act seemingly most brutal and gratuitous, Brown has, somehow, in a last distortion, affirmed himself as human, not brute, has affirmed, paradoxically, the human need for moral vindication. And let us not forget that Jim, the redeemed, had confronted Brown, the damned, in a dark dialogue of communion and complicity delivered back and forth across a jungle creek.

Each of us longs for full balance and responsibility in self-knowledge, in a recognition and harmonious acceptance of our destiny. Saints and sages may achieve that harmonious sense of destiny, or the hero at the cannon-mouth, or the famous sergeant of Belleau Wood. But we lesser and more fumbling mortals may find at least some intimation of it in the unfolding pattern, however modest, of our own effort toward knowledge.

I know that this has been a congress of philosophers, and I have a becoming diffidence about offering my amateur and homemade product after the three-day exhibit of glittering articles. If I am invited here at all, it is with the credentials of one who tries to write novels and poems and not of one who tries to philosophize. And that would suggest that the thing I was supposed to do in the first place was to remark on what relation I find between my own profession and the topic of this meeting. So I'll say my say, though I find myself saying it in the last, not the first, place. But last place may be best, for what has gone before, if it has accomplished anything, will explain what now I try to say.

I'll start by making one of the most debatable statements one can make: Poetry — that is, literature as a dimension of the creative imagination — is knowledge.

In accidental or incidental ways, poetry may, of course, give knowledge, even very important knowledge, but I do not mean such accidental or incidental knowledge. I do not mean, for instance, the absurdity I now shall tell you about, an absurdity we have all encountered in many places but which I have most recently encountered in a philosophical journal. The author of this absurdity, who no doubt embarrasses his friends, announces himself as a logical positivist, then argues that the novel is the most valuable form of art, for some novels give valid historical, sociological, and psychological knowledge. True, all novels report human motives and actions, and the settings, spatial, temporal, and social, in which those actions take place. But such reports occur much more systematically in works of history, geography, psychology, etc., and most certainly cannot be taken as the thing that characterizes and differentiates the novel as an art form. No, the novel, as novel, as art-form, is not reporting anything — how to drive chariots or govern cities. It is using certain materials, which may include valid knowledge of chariot-driving or city-government, for its characteristic purposes, etc. There is no use to pursue the argument. Let us blush, avert our eyes, and pass on from this scene of logical naiveté and terminological carnage and Hobbesian nonsense. In other words, knowledge by report is not the kind of knowledge I mean in this discussion.

Nor do I mean what, for lack of a better term, we may call knowledge by symptom, the knowledge we may get from a work by regarding it as a cultural or linguistic symptom, or the symptom of its age or author. True, we may learn much by regarding poetry as symptom — for example, about an age or author, if we know how to take the deep ambivalences, the condensations, the subtle distortions and essential purgations of an age or personality. But again, such knowledge is not characteristic or differentiating.

If knowledge by report and knowledge by symptom, however valuable and interesting such knowledge may be, are not characteristic and differentiating, then what kind of knowledge am I talking about? I should say: knowledge by form. No, knowledge *of* form.

By this I mean the furthest thing possible from any doctrine that might go as sheer formalism. I mean the organic relation among all the elements of the work, including, *most emphatically*, those elements drawn from the actual world and charged with all the urgencies of actuality, urgencies not to be denied but transmuted — as we are told Tintoretto transmuted the gamin divers of the Venetian canals into the angels of his painting. The form is a vision of experience, but of experience fulfilled and redeemed in knowledge, the ugly with the beautiful, the slayer with the slain, what was known as shape now known as time, what was known in time now known as shape, a new knowledge. It is not a thing detached from the world but a thing springing from the deep engagement of spirit with the world. This engagement may involve not only love for the world, but also fear and disgust, but the conquest, in form, of fear and disgust means such a sublimation that the world which once provoked the fear and disgust may now be totally loved in the fulness of contemplation. The form is the flowering of that deep engagement of spirit, the discovery of its rhythm. And the form is known, by creator or appreciator, only by experiencing it, by submitting to its characteristic rhythm.

With this word *rhythm*, I am reminded of the necessary question: how does the knowledge of form give man an image of himself?

It does so insofar as it gives the image of experience being brought to order and harmony, the image of a dance on the high wire over an abyss. The rhythm is, as it were, a myth of order, or fulfillment, an affirmation that our being may move in its totality toward meaning. The soul faces some potentiality of experience, drawn from actuality, and the form is the flowing vibration of the soul, the abstraction of experience by imagination. The form gives man an image of himself for it gives him his mode of experiencing, a paradigm of his inner life, his rhythm of destiny, his tonality of fate. And this evocation, confrontation, and definition of our deepest life gives us, in new self-awareness, a yet deeper life to live.

But not merely the life of contemplation, for the soul does not sit in self-regarding trance, like Rachel before her mirror all the day, in Dante's *Purgatorio*. No, that gazing prepares for the moment of action, of creation, in our world of contingency. It is, as Yeats puts it,

> . . . Our secret discipline
> Wherein the gazing soul doubles her might.

The might is there for the moment when the soul lifts her head.

Rod W. Horton and Herbert W. Edwards

From Evolution and Pragmatism

As has been pointed out, these two branches of study [philosophy and theology] were in 1850 still pretty much the same thing. Perhaps the most fundamental area of agreement between them was in

Reprinted from *Backgrounds of American Literary Thought*, Rod W. Horton and Herbert W. Edwards, eds., 2nd ed (New York: Meredith Publishing Company, 1967), pp. 54-58. Copyright © 1967 by Meredith Publishing Company.

regard to the nature of truth, which was assumed to have existed *a priori* (from the beginning) eternal, unchanging, and divine in essence. Opinion had differed from time to time as to just how much of this truth could possibly be known to the mind of man, but its nature and its absolute finality were rarely questioned by philosophy and never by theology. For the latter this conception of truth was inescapable, since God is by definition the source of all truth. To the theological mind Truth is always capitalized, and exists as some remote and hitherto unscaled peak of ultimate knowledge which has always existed and will some day yield its ultimate secret to the mind of man. The religious view in general was that such revelation would not come this side of the grave, except in rare and mystical moments of exaltation incommunicable to others. But since man's idea of Truth is a reflection, however dim and distorted, of the eternal and unchanging Truth in the mind of a Perfect Knower, ultimate revelation must come, whether in this world or the next.

To supplant this way of thinking, weighted with the authority of centuries of unquestioning acceptance, William James proposed the basic principles of pragmatism:

1. That the world not only *seems* to be spontaneous, discontinuous and unpredictable, but that it actually *is*.
2. That truth is not inherent *in* ideas, but is something that happens *to* ideas in the process of being used in real-life situations.
3. That man is free to believe what he *wills* to believe about the world, so long as his belief does not contradict either his practical experience or his scientific knowledge.
4. That the ultimate value of truth is not as a point of rest upon absolute certainty, but solely in its power to lead us to still other truths about the world we live in.

Thus James had achieved at one stroke a philosophical view of the world that was essentially in accord with the common sense opinion of the ordinary man and yet left room for him in the universe as a free and responsible agent, working out his problems through the use of his practical intelligence. All experience is real, he held, but man is not required to deal with all of it at once or even to explain all of it at once. Sufficient unto the particular situation is the truth that "works" for that situation. If it is a genuine *pragmatic* truth, it will also direct us toward the steps in solving the next problem.

This line of reasoning brought philosophy down from its ivory tower with a vengeance. To the average man, who by force of circumstance has always been more or less of a pragmatist, these ideas may seem obvious enough, but to the generally idealistic philosophers of the mid-nineteenth century the effect was shattering. For centuries they had been stubbornly selecting out of the context of total experience certain favored elements or factors which were "true" and "good" and assigning relatively inferior and even illusory status to those elements which refused to conform to the grand design. Now it was as though one end of this age-old tug-of-war between appearance and reality in the universe had been suddenly let go, and the philosophers, like Othello, were all at once without an occupation. If *all* experience is equally "real" and "true," they said in dismay, then the world is chaos and no longer the concern of philosophers. To the first proposition James cheerfully assented but to the second he returned an emphatic negative.

Pragmatism, he said, is both a philosophy and a philosophical method. As a philosophy it postulates a discontinuously evolving universe in which man is one element among many. As a method it is inductive, scientific, non-absolutist, and based on the principle that the final test of the truth or falsity of an idea is the actual difference it will make when applied to a concrete, practical situation. No idea is to be regarded as "true" once and for all. Further, we should stand ready to revise our entire framework of ideas, should tomorrow's scientific discoveries require it. To pragmatism, this central principle, namely, that our beliefs are in reality rules of action, and must be tested by their practical consequences, is the keystone of the arch. Equally basic to James's system is his recognition of the psychological fact that to a large extent man believes what he *wants* to believe. Ideas unmotivated by the will to act are stillborn; but before man acts beyond the minimum necessary to sustain life he must have a mental picture of the possible results of his action that will be sufficiently attractive to make him *want* to act. Such a mental picture is compounded in part of his actual knowledge, based on past experience, and his human desire to bring about certain consequences rather than others.

Thus, applying James's own pragmatic test, man may have free will simply by choosing to believe that he does have it, because in a given real-life situation the practical results will be different if he so believes. To a people who had subdued an entire continent in a century such an idea would appear only the plainest common sense. After all, Emerson had said almost the same thing a generation earlier, and many of those who had "hitched their wagon to a star" had bent and shaped the world to their heart's desire. True, many more had not; but Americans in 1890 still used the exceptions to prove the rule of rags to riches through luck and pluck, and still retained enough of Emerson's moral idealism to believe that the new world they were creating would infallibly be a better one. James's willingness to dignify such wishful thinking by including it in pragmatism confounded the orthodox of both classroom and pulpit. How, they asked, could a rigorously intellectual discipline like philosophy have anything to do with the irrational and disrupting chaos of human desires, fears, wants, and satisfactions? James's reply was simply that it always had been so. Even the most absolute idealists of the past, he pointed out, had selected as their eternal and unchanging truths only those aspects of the universe that fit in most satisfactorily with their point of view. Contradictory evidence they simply ignored or viewed as evil.

For his part, James was ready to admit even religion into philosophy so long as it had a demonstrable effect upon man's decisions to act in one way rather than another. Indeed, James's interest in religion was of the keenest, and he devoted one entire book to a study of its pyschological effects [*Varieties of Religious Experience* (1902)]. In his own phrase, he was a *radical* empiricist, not limited to verifiable sense data alone, but ready to consider everything that fell within the range of human experience. Since it was obvious to James that religious considerations *do* affect men's actions, then pragmatism was bound to regard religion as just as much of a reality as the stone or wood of the churches themselves.

Unfortunately for the clergy, who might otherwise have welcomed James's support, pragmatism's concept of God and the universe was unorthodox in the extreme. What religious leader of James's day — or our own — could subscribe to an "Apostles' Creed" that goes like this:

> Suppose that the world's author put the case to you before creation, saying: "I am going to make a world not certain to be saved, a world the perfection of which shall be conditional merely, the condition being that each several agent does its own 'level best.' I offer you the chance of taking part in such a world. Its safety, you see, is unwarranted. It is a real adventure, with real danger, yet it may win through. It is a social scheme of co-operative work genuinely to be done. Will you join the procession? Will you trust yourself and trust the other agents enough to face the risk?" [1]

And it is entirely characteristic of James that he goes on to state in the next paragraph that he believes that most "healthy-minded, buoyant people" would say "yes" to such a proposition, because it is "just like the world we practically live in; and loyalty to our old

---

[1] William James, *Pragmatism Selections* (1949), Chapt. v, "Pragmatism and Religion," 93. Used by permission of Paul R. Reynolds.

nurse Nature would forbid us to say 'no.' " Such a world, he says, "would seem 'rational' to us in the most living way."

This stirring call to the strenuous life, so reminiscent of Teddy Roosevelt and the charge up San Juan Hill, is evidence that even in a religious context, pragmatism was completely and characteristically American. As James shrewdly assumed, his picture of an open universe, full of interesting possibilities and not fundamentally hostile to man's concerns, was a realistic approximation of what the average man actually believed. God remained as a vaguely benevolent Force, but one not so necessary as formerly and content to let a multitude of confusing and sometimes antagonistic factors work themselves out to the general betterment of mankind. Practically no one believed any longer in Calvinistic predestination, and few were concerned with defining the exact limits of Divine and human causation. They looked out upon a vast and spacious universe with time enough and to spare for any and all projects that scientific social planning might suggest. World War I, the disillusion of the Twenties, the Depression, World War II—all these lay in the future. For the moment, it was sufficient that in pragmatism William James had formulated a philosophy that even the man in the street could recognize as relevant to the concerns of his daily life. . . .

John Milton

From *Paradise Lost*

> Now had th' Almighty Father from above,
> From the pure empyrean where he sits
> High throned above all height, bent down his eye,
> His own works and their works at once to view:
> About him all the sanctities of Heaven
> Stood thick as stars, and from his sight received
> Beatitude past utterance; on his right
> The radiant image of his glory sat,
> His only Son. On Earth he first beheld
> Our two first parents, yet the only two

Book III, 11. 56-134.

Of mankind, in the happy garden placed,
Reaping immortal fruits of joy and love,
Uninterrupted joy, unrivaled love,
In blissful solitude. He then surveyed
Hell and the gulf between, and Satan there
Coasting the wall of Heaven on this side Night,
In the dun air sublime, and ready now
To stoop, with wearied wings and willing feet,
On the bare outside of this world, that seemed
Firm land embosomed without firmament,
Uncertain which, in ocean or in air.
Him God beholding from his prospect high,
Wherein past, present, future, he beholds,
Thus to his only Son foreseeing spake:
   "Only-begotten Son, seest thou what rage
Transports our adversary? whom no bounds
Prescribed, no bars of Hell, nor all the chains
Heaped on him there, nor yet the main abyss
Wide interrupt, can hold; so bent he seems
On desperate revenge, that shall redound
Upon his own rebellious head. And now,
Through all restraint broke loose, he wings his way
Not far off Heaven, in the precincts of light,
Directly towards the new-created world,
And man there placed, with purpose to essay
If him by force he can destroy, or, worse,
By some false guile pervert: and shall pervert;
For man will hearken to his glozing lies,
And easily transgress the sole command,
Sole pledge of his obedience; so will fall
He and his faithless progeny. Whose fault?
Whose but his own? Ingrate, he had of me
All he could have; I made him just and right,
Sufficient to have stood, though free to fall.
Such I created all th' ethereal powers
And spirits, both them who stood and them who failed:
Freely they stood who stood, and fell who fell.
Not free, what proof could they have given sincere
Of true allegiance, constant faith, or love,
Where only what they needs must do appeared,
Not what they would? What praise could they receive,
What pleasure I, from such obedience paid,
When Will and Reason (Reason also is Choice),

Useless and vain, of freedom both despoiled,
Made passive both, had served Necessity,
Not me? They, therefore, as to right belonged,
So were created, nor can justly accuse
Their Maker, or their making, or their fate,
As if predestination overruled
Their will, disposed by absolute decree
Or high foreknowledge. They themselves decreed
Their own revolt, not I. If I foreknew,
Foreknowledge had no influence on their fault,
Which had no less proved certain unforeknown.
So without least impulse or shadow of fate,
Or aught by me immutably foreseen,
They trespass, authors to themselves in all,
Both what they judge and what they choose; for so
I informed them free, and free they must remain
Till they enthrall themselves: I else must change
Their nature, and revoke the high decree
Unchangeable, eternal, which ordained
Their freedom; they themselves ordained their fall.
The first sort by their own suggestion fall,
Self-tempted, self-depraved; man falls, deceived
By the other first: man, therefore, shall find grace;
The other, none. In mercy and justice both,
Through Heaven and Earth, so shall my glory excel;
But mercy, first and last, shall brightest shine."

Charles Kaplan

Jack Burden: Modern Ishmael

The story is told in the first person by a young man who has something of importance to tell us about his past experiences. In order to communicate the meaning of those experiences, he has to make us relive them with him. Consequently, he does not flatly and inartisti-

Reprinted from *College English*, XXII (October, 1960), 19-24,'by permission of the National Council of Teachers of English and the author. Copyright © 1960 by the National Council of Teachers of English.

cally give away the "ending", instead, he recreates his adventures retrospectively, both as a means of defining to himself the nature of what has happened to him and as a means of dramatically involving the passive reader. As he tells the narrative, he finds himself faced with the usual kinds of technical difficulties which writers of fiction must resolve: the vantage-point of the narrator, the relevant incidents, the sequence of those incidents, the problems of foreshortening and focusing, the symbols, the language and the tone, and so on. The young man adopts a narrative strategy designed to evoke the desired effect in his readers.

Briefly summarized, his story revolves about a crisis in his life, during which time he comes under the influence of an almost superhumanly powerful personality in a position of unchallengeable authority. As the narrator tells the story, he himself seems to become a secondary participant or even fade from the picture, and the strong authoritarian individual grows until he dominates the scene completely. This man, perfectly at home in his world, expresses his attitude toward it by towering contemptuously above his fellow-creatures. For him, understanding has led not to humility but to arrogance. His behavior reveals assumptions concerning his own infallibility, as he begins to play God and to impose his own ideas about the world on intractable nature. The consequence of such colossal pride is downfall and death. But the young man, watching and reporting this career, undergoes a significant change: as the stronger figure loses contact with humanity, eventually to die, the narrator moves in a reverse pattern, eventually to be reintegrated, to rejoin the world of human beings from which he had originally felt himself alienated. Or, to use a more precise figure of speech which the narrator himself supplies, he is "reborn."

The faceless account given above will naturally suggest to many readers the plan of *Moby Dick*. But, in the words of W. H. Auden, "Most American books might well start like *Moby Dick*. 'Call me Ishmael' . . . . Most American novels are parables, their settings even when they pretend to be realistic, symbolic settings for a timeless and unlocated (because internal) psychomachia." Overlooking the sweeping quality of Auden's observation, it is certainly true that in at least one very striking instance, the anonymous narrator whom we know only as Ishmael has a prototype in a well-known and widely-read modern "realistic" novel: Robert Penn Warren's *All the King's Men*.

One of the reasons for the continuing popular success of Warren's novel since its appearance in 1946 (when it won the Pulitzer Prize) has been its recognizable politico-historical basis, as well as the rapid and melodramatic plot itself. The era of Huey Long is not so far behind us that the *roman a clef* element can be totally disregarded; furthermore, as a sociological study of Southern political types and particularly of the American agrarian demagogue, the accuracy of Warren's rendering is noteworthy, and reminds us forcibly of the real world in which we exist.[1] Both the Academy Award-winning motion picture version of the novel and the stage version stress the element emphasized on the cover of the paperback edition: "The world-famous American novel of power and corruption, and the meteoric rise and fall of Willie Stark — politician."

But it is as misleading to let this stand as a complete description of *All the King's Men* as it would be to say that *Moby Dick* is a novel about whaling, or that *Hamlet* is a play about a young man who kills his uncle. Jack Burden, Warren's "Ishmael," at the end acknowledges the double nature of the tale he has told:

> This has been the story of Willie Stark, but it is my story too. For I have a story. It is the story of a man who lived in the world and to him the world looked one way for a long time and then it looked another and very different way. The change did not happen all at once. Many things happened, and that man did not know when he had any responsibility for them and when he did not. There was, in fact, a time when he came to believe that nobody had any responsibility for anything and there was no god but the Great Twitch.

But as Jack Burden moves and struggles in the world of Willie Stark he eventually comes to accept the responsibility of being a human being, a responsibility which means involvement in "the convulsion of the world." The novel concludes "in the summer of this year, 1939," with Jack Burden finally ready to share the human burden as a mature and responsible adult. The events which began in late summer, 1939, suggest the world convulsion which Jack is now able to confront responsibly. An understanding of the world, a readiness to be engaged in it (instead of shrinking from it and interpreting everything as the meaningless Great Twitch), depends on understanding one's self — and this is what has happened to Jack.

A similar change takes place in Ishmael, although less explicitly defined. The opening paragraph of *Moby Dick* depicts his condition prior to sailing on the Pequod. It is a period of the "damp, drizzly November" in his soul, when he is "grim about the mouth" and finds himself "involuntarily pausing before coffin warehouses, and bring-

---

[1] An article dealing with this aspect of the novel is *"All the King's Men*: A Study in Populism," by Malcolm O. Sillars, in *American Quarterly*, Fall, 1957.

ing up the rear of every funeral" he meets. The gloomy, life-despairing Ishmael finds reflections of his own isolation everywhere he looks, in "the insular city of the "Manhattoes" and the Pequod as well — "Isolatoes too, I call such, not acknowledging the common continent of men, but each Isolato living on a separate continent of his own." The double pattern of action thereafter is to show Ishmael gradually rediscovering this common continent, while Ahab, in gaining diabolical control over his crewmen, alienates himself from mankind and is doomed to a "desolation of solitude" until his death.

Ishmael's progress in rediscovering the common continent is marked by several key incidents in the narrative. At first terror-stricken and horrified by being thrown together with the pagan Queequeg, apparently as unlikely a representative of average humanity as one could hope to encounter, Ishmael soon discovers qualities of sociability, friendship, and love binding them together. And when Queequeg proffers his pipe and says that henceforth they are "married; meaning in his country's phrase, that we were bosom friends; he would gladly die for me, if need should be," Ishmael is no longer alone. (It is, significantly, Queequeg's buoyant coffin that paradoxically gives Ishmael life after the Pequod is sunk.) In the scene of the monkey-rope, when Queequeg and Ishmael are tied together while the harpooner dispatches a whale down in the ocean, Ishmael's reflection is that Queequeg is his "own inseparable twin brother; nor could I any way get rid of the dangerous liabilities which the hempen bond entailed." Brotherhood and responsibility are bonds, but they also may involve dangerous obligations from which man cannot shrink. Both Ishmael and Jack Burden make this crucial discovery which results in their salvation, while Ahab and Willie Stark refuse to acknowledge it as truth. In a later scene which dramatizes the Dickinson aphorism, "Much madness is divinest sense," Ishmael sits with his crewmates squeezing lumps of sperm into fluid. This mindless occupation gradually arouses in him "abounding, affectionate, friendly, loving" feelings, so that "at last I was continually squeezing their hands and looking up into their eyes sentimentally; as much as to say, — Oh! my dear fellow beings, why should we longer cherish any social acerbities, or know the slightest ill-humor or envy! Come; let us squeeze hands all around; nay, let us all squeeze ourselves into each other; let us squeeze ourselves universally into the very milk and sperm of kindness." The episode in which Ishmael, hypnotized by the fierce glare of the try-works, falls asleep at the tiller and reverses his position, turning his back to the compass, dramatizes Ahab's permanent posture, for Ahab is a man who has looked too long in the face of the fire, a man

who has discarded quadrant and compass. Ishmael quotes the words
of Solomon: "The man that wandereth out of the way of understanding shall remain in the congregation of the dead." It is Ishmael's fate
—but not Ahab's—to return to the congregation of the living. After
the Pequod goes down, Ishmael floats "on a soft and dirge-like
main," unharmed by sharks and savage sea-hawks, until he is rescued by "the devious-cruising Rachel, that in her retracing search
after her missing children, only found another orphan." Ishmael is
brought back to the family of man. His experience at sea under Captain Ahab has been one of self-discovery; figuratively, he is reborn
and (literally, also) he is saved.

Jack Burden is a student of history who balks at understanding
the past; he sees the experience but refuses to accept the meaning in
the story of Cass Mastern, his Ph.D. dissertation topic. As a result
of his refusal to face what the facts tell him, Jack drifts off into a
career of irresponsible isolationism, although ostensibly participat-
ing actively in the world as Willie Stark's assistant and leg-man.
Much later, Jack faces the meaning of the Cass Mastern story:

> Cass Mastern lived for a few years and in that time he learned that
> the world is all of one piece. He learned that the world is like an
> enormous spider web and if you touch it, however lightly, at any
> point, the vibration ripples to the remotest perimeter and the drowsy
> spider feels the tingle and is drowsy no more but springs out to fling
> the gossamer coils about you who have touched the web and then
> inject the black, numbing poison under your hide. It does not matter
> whether or not you meant to brush the web of things.

It is this sense of involvement, of the complexity of human relation-
ships in a highly complex world, that Jack Burden flees from. To
him it is a "monstrous conspiracy," and he takes refuge in one of
his recurring periods of escapism to which he gives the name of the
Great Sleep. Jack refuses to acknowledge his comon humanity; that
is, he acknowledges the presence of ugliness and evil in the universe
but insists on his own separateness and aloofness from them. He
does not shrink from evil, but he refuses to see that in order to be
human he must acknowledge the evil and guilt within himself. Like
Cass Mastern, he eventually learns that man cannot escape guilt,
even an unintended guilt.

Who killed Willie Stark? It was Dr. Adam Stanton, of course, who
fired the gun; but all — Adam, Tiny Duffy, Anne Stanton, Sadie
Burke, and Jack himself (not to omit Willie) — are partly responsible. It is a shared guilt, the vibrations of the spider web involving
all of them. What shocks Jack most of all is that his role is unin-

tended; that is, in the interests of sterile factual research, he has also been responsible for Willie's murder. "It was as though I were caught in a more monstrous conspiracy whose meaning I could not fathom." After Willie's death, with Jack unwilling to accept the implications of his role, "I hated everything and everybody and myself and Tiny Duffy and Willie Stark and Adam Stanton. To hell with them all, I said impartially under the stars. They all looked alike to me then. And I looked like them." This recognition of his basic identification with the rest of ugly, corrupt, and incomplete humanity is what Jack Burden is struggling against.

Throughout the novel Jack takes refuge in a state of not-knowing, the Great Sleep being simply one variation. In the first chapter, he describes a state of tense anticipation using the image of a foetus:

> It wants to lie in the dark and not know, and be warm in its not-knowing. The end of man is knowledge, but there is one thing he can't know: whether knowledge will save him or kill him.

But man has to "open the envelope" in any event, "for the end of man is to know." Later, after learning of Willie's affair with Anne, Jack flees to California, in an automatic gesture of recoil, "because when you don't like it where you are you always go west . . . . That was why I drowned in West." That this drowning, another attempt to return to the womb-state, solves no problems is evidenced by the fact that when he returns he still feels "at one with the Great Twitch" in a world where actions are neither good nor evil but meaningless, in a world out of time. As a history student who refuses to accept the past and who does not know his own past, Jack can have no concern about the future, and therefore the present is also meaningless. Jack creates his own insulated, sheltered, womb-state world.

That world, however, is crackled open when Jack Burden hears his mother scream one night — "a bright, beautiful, silvery soprano scream. I bounced off the bed and started for the door, realized that I was buck-naked, grabbed a robe, and ran out." Her involuntary cry of pain occurs when she finds that Jack's real father, Judge Irwin, has committed suicide (one of the other results of Jack's neutral "research"), and she accuses Jack of killing his father. But this moment inaugurates a change in Jack's vision of the world. Jack's rebirth is traumatic, but it begins to give him a new picture of his father (or rather gives him a picture of his new father) and a new understanding of his mother as a woman with a greater capacity for love than he had been willing to grant, rather than one "who loved merely power over men and the momentary satisfaction to vanity or flesh which they could give her, who lived in a strange loveless oscillation between calculation and instinct." What this rediscovery of his mother means is that, by giving him a new picture of herself, she can give him back the past "which I had before felt was tainted and horrible. I could accept the past now because I could accept her and be at peace with her and with myself." Jack's increase in understanding and acceptance of the world enables him also to be at peace with the Scholarly Attorney, the man he had previously thought was his father. When he discovers their true relationship, he can begin to accept the old man on altered terms, in a way that he could not before. Jack's reintegration is complete.

"There are two ways," Reinhold Niebuhr writes, "of denying our responsibilities to our fellowmen. The one is the way of imperialism, expressed in seeking to dominate them by our power. The other way is the way of isolationism, expressed in seeking to withdraw from our responsibilities to them." The irresponsibility of Jack Burden is an example of the latter kind; Willie Stark is clearly the example of domination. But what is the cause of Willie's downfall? It is, ironically, his "idealistic" decision to build a memorial hospital to his son Tom, free of the taint of such corrupt and grafting henchmen as Tiny Duffy and Gummy Larson. The key principle in Willie's career has been his recognition of the inseparability of abstrations like "good" and "evil," of the rejection of moral absolutes. He tells Adam Stanton that "goodness" has to be made "out of badness . . . And you know why? Because there isn't anything else to make it out of." Or, as he is fond of saying: "Man is conceived in sin and born in corruption and he passeth from the stink of the didie to the stench of the shroud." But Tom's death causes him to forget his guiding principle, and he becomes the victim of his attempt to divorce idealistic aspiration from brute corruption. Willie's monomaniacal obsession is of shorter duration and is less pervasive than Ahab's, but both are embodiments of the demon-ridden personality seeking transcedent absolutes. Each seeks to impose his own ideal upon nature; in so doing each alienates himself from common humanity and dies.

One of the reasons for the success of *All the King's Men*, as pointed out earlier, is the "realistic" picture of southern statehouse politics. Warren's novel is full of that "solidity of specification" which Henry James insisted on, "that merit on which all its other merits . . . helplessly and submissively depend." Likewise, one of the basic qualities in *Moby Dick* (in addition to the element of excitement in the hunting of the whale) is that enumeration of factual detail found most obviously (but not exclusively) in the cetological chapters which have raised so many finicky critical eyebrows. These are recognizable every-day worlds created and inhabited by their narrators; the legislative machinations or whaling pursuits serve to define the principal boundaries and activities of those worlds. If the significance of the narrator's experience is that he sees meaning in rejoining the real world of human beings, then it is up to the artist to bring that world to life.

The rhetorical shifts which both authors employ as part of their strategy are also remarkably similar. Jack Burden's language alternates between the dry, unemotional reporting of the detached observer and the almost lyrical introspection of the tortured but ironical victim. In the former style, it is almost a parody of Hemingway:

> I hung the receiver up very deliberately, walked over to the desk and asked the clerk to give my bag to a bellhop, got a drink out of the lobby cooler, bought a couple of packs of cigarettes from the sleepy sister at the lobby stand, opened a package and lighted myself one, and stood there to take a long drag and look at the blank lobby, as though there weren't any place in the world where I had to go.

But this is Jack Burden, passive on his hotel bed, recapitulating history as he attempts to "drown in West":

> For that is where you come, after you have crossed oceans and eaten stale biscuits while prisoned forty days and nights in a stormy-tossed rat-trap, after you have sweated in the greenery and heard the savage whoop, after you have built cabins and cities and bridged rivers, after you have lain with women and scattered children like millet seed in a high wind, after you have composed resonant documents, made noble speeches, and bathed your arms in blood to the elbows, after you have shaken with malaria in the marshes and in the icy wind across the high plains. That is where you come, to lie alone on a bed in a hotel room in Long Beach, California. There I lay, while outside my window a neon sign flickered on and off to the time of my heart, systole and diastole, flushing and flushing again the gray sea mist with a tint like blood.

It is important to note that the present Jack Burden, who recalls the old Jack Burden, is employing alternating styles in order to recreate and embody the two aspects of that un-integrated personality. Seeing himself as from a distance, he even shifts pronouns in the long sequence dealing with Jack Burden's university career, where it is not "I" but "he" — the epitome of detachment.

The stylistic devices which Melville makes available to Ishmael range also from factual registering of details concerning whale anatomy and the whaling industry to the Elizabethan rhetoric of the dramatic soliloquies. It is not literal verisimilitude but imaginative suggestiveness that Ishmael is aiming for; consequently, in his reconstruction of the whaling world he even includes incidents which, strictly speaking, he cannot have seen. But these imaginative touches constitute the liberty which an artist is entitled to take in order to make more fully comprehensive the symbolic nature of his experience.

I do not suggest that Warren went to Melville for his model, either consciously or unconsciously. But in the light of the remarkable parallelisms between the two novels, the more than hundred years of time between them seem little enough barrier to establish their family resemblance. Ishmael and Jack Burden recreate for us an archetypal pattern of human behavior, moving, as Aristotle has it, from ignorance to knowledge — "the end of man is to know" — or from isolation to common cause with mankind. The fate of the proud man who steps outside of what Hawthorne called "the magnetic chain of humanity" is isolation, perhaps temporary dominion and giddying power, but also self-torture and painful death. The fate of the Ishmael-outcast who picks up his burden of human responsibilities and re-enters the magnetic field is rebirth, love, and life.

Ted N. Weissbuch

Jack Burden: Call Me Carraway

In "Jack Burden: Modern Ishmael" (*College English*, October, 1960), Dr. Charles Kaplan suggests that Melville's Ishmael has a

Reprinted from *College English*, XXII (February, 1961), 361, by permission of the National Council of Teachers of English. Copyright © 1961 by the National Council of Teachers of English.

prototype in Jack Burden, narrator of Robert Penn Warren's *All The King's Men*. While many similarities exist in both characters, Jack Burden is more like Nick Carraway, the narrator in Fitzgerald's *The Great Gatsby* (1925). It is not my intention to attack the Ishmael-Burden thesis, but rather to suggest that Burden's literary ancestry may be located closer at hand than Professor Kaplan suggests. His quotation from W. H. Auden, that "Most American books might well start like *Moby Dick* . . . 'Call me Ishmael,' " is closer to the truth than the theory of the Ishmael-Burden relationship. Perhaps it is the universality of *Moby Dick* which helps to explain its greatness.

Several other authors and novels come to mind in terms of focus, technique, and plot. Robert C. Slack has related Jack Burden's story to the Telemachus theme, the dispossessed young man on a spiritual quest for the purpose of finding his "father," and re-establishing contact with his home, community, and world. Tyler Spotswood, narrator of John Dos Passos's *Number One*, which appeared in 1943, three years before the Warren novel, is the same type of observer-participant in the story of a Southern demagogue forcing his will on the public by means of bureaucratic control. This similarity is discussed in *All The King's Men: A Symposium*, by Members of the Department of English, Carnegie Institute of Technology, 1957. The Telemachus theme also appears in James Joyce, Thomas Wolfe, Eugene O'Neill, T. S. Eliot, and Willa Cather. Coincidentally, the narrator's name in Miss Cather's *My Antonia* (1918), is Jim Burden; like Jack Burden and Nick Carraway, he is also concerned with his involvement in history and time. In the last pages of Miss Cather's novel, Jim Burden tells Antonia that no matter what they have missed, they have possessed together "the precious, the incommunicable past." After twenty years of separation, he experiences his "rebirth."

But Warren's Jack Burden and Carraway, in the last analysis, offer the greatest similarities. Burden accepts the responsibility of returning "into the convulsion of the world, out of history into history and the awful responsibility of Time." Carraway also emphasizes the time-history relationship in trying to understand the world. Just as Burden's character develops only after he accepts his heritage, his past, and a sense of responsibility, so Nick grows when he realizes that Gatsby's dream of the green light across the bay is the "orgiastic future that year by year recedes before us. . . . So we beat on, boats against the current, borne back ceaselessly into the past." Both informants retain their socially elevated positions and emerge from their narratives embittered but matured.

Each develops a sense of acceptance based on his willingness to face the world on its own terms. Carraway comes to realize that the East Egg-West Egg futility and falseness permeate not only the surface of Gatsby's life, but the entire culture. This cynical insight results in his statement that Gatsby is "worth the whole damn bunch put together." Burden's "moral neutrality of history" emerges when he realizes that "history is blind, but man is not," and that "in the end the truth gave the past back to me." While Professor Kaplan's thesis is correct in pointing to similarities between Ishmael and Burden, I submit that the latter's ancestry can be traced to a whole series of "reborn" characters who are closer to him in time, perception, and subject matter than is Ishmael.

L. Hugh Moore, Jr.

Robert Penn Warren and The Terror of Answered Prayer

Robert Penn Warren learned Italian in order to read Dante; he used a passage from *The Divine Comedy* as an epigraph to *All the King's Men*, and he has said that the seventh circle of *The Inferno* provided the plan of *At Heaven's Gate* — the characters are, like Dante's, violent against self, nature, or God. Also, it is becoming increasingly apparent that the scope of Warren's work can be compared to Dante's. His novels and poetry, like Dante's epic, add up to a profound spiritual pilgrimage with relevant comments upon morals, manners, and society. Warren has created his Hell in *Night Rider* and *At Heaven's Gate*, his Purgatory in *All the King's Men and World Enough and Time*, and his Heaven, at least in brief glimpses, in *Brother to Dragons*, *Wilderness*, and more personally in *Promises*.

It is, then, hardly surprising to discover one of Dante's main themes, one that determines the structures of much of *The Divine*

Reprinted from *Mississippi Quarterly*, XXI (Winter, 1967-68), 29-36, by permission of the publisher and the author.

Comedy, deeply embedded in Warren's work. This theme is that man usually gets what he wants and asks for, that Divine Justice answers prayers. No one is sent to Hell in Dante's plan. The damned choose it freely, and their punishment is the sin, or its result, in its essential nature for all eternity. Thus their desires are requited. Dorothy Sayers explains that "Neither in the *story* nor in the *allegory* is Hell a place of punishment to which anyone is sent; it is the condition to which the soul reduces itself by a stubborn determination to evil, and in which it suffers the torment of its own perversions."[1] Paolo and Francesca are together, as they wished, through all eternity but still, as on earth, buffeted by the winds of passion. Now, however, their only desires are for rest and peace which they have forever forfeited. Jack Burden toward the end of the novel in which he describes his own descent into Hell puts the same idea in his own characteristic idiom: "My only crime was being a man and living in the world of men, and you don't have to do special penance for that. That crime and the penance, in that case, coincide perfectly, they are identical."[2]

Many of Warren's characters are, like Dante's, the victims of disordered desires that lead them to want the wrong things. Often, too, as in *The Inferno*, they achieve their own Hell by getting exactly what they want. This scheme is well suited to Warren's use of irony. More basically and inevitably, it ties in precisely with two of his main preoccupations: the corrupt nature of man and the enormous complexity of the world. These are the reasons men have wrong goals and desires, why they choose Hell even at Heaven's Gate. In Warren's cosmology the world often grants wishes, not because there is, as in Dante, a clear moral order inherent in the universe, but chiefly, it seems, because of chance, the blind flux of events that can yield tragic irony. Getting one's desires is, to Warren, merely another one of the risks inherent in the human condition. The world of Robert Penn Warren, thus, seems to have a moral order like that of *The Divine Comedy.*

Many of Warren's characters harbor disordered desires because of innate depravity, "the taint in the bloodstream," a propensity to evil which Warren often calls by its theological name Original Sin, the sin of self of which all are guilty. Deficient in self-knowledge, these people fail to realize that they, like the worst of sinners, are

---

[1] Dorothy L. Sayers, Introduction to *The Comedy of Dante Alighieri* (Baltimore, 1948), p. 68.

[2] Robert Penn Warren, *All the King's Men* (New York, 1946), p. 358. All subsequent references to *All the King's Men* are to this edition.

brother to dragons. MacCarland Sumpter in *The Cave* discovers that the terror of God is that He answers prayers, even unspoken ones that spring from the inner recesses of the depraved self.

> . . . MacCarland Sumpter shook with his first knowledge of the dark deviousness of that God Who knows how to wait. The terror of God is that God conforms His will to man's will. The terror of God is that He bends ear to man's prayer. Knock and it shall be opened unto you. And when it is opened, who can withstand the horror of that vision of prayer fulfilled? [3]

Reverend Sumpter lives in an agonized Hell of guilt because of his unspoken and unrecognized wish that Jack Harrick's baby which his wife was carrying before their marriage not live to offend his pride by being an eternal reminder that Jack and not he who nobly married her was the one to introduce her to passion. His prayer is answered, for the baby dies. Later, he prays that the search for the trapped Jasper will save his own son, Isaac, by giving him the opportunity to display the virtues of courage and self-sacrifice, virtues hitherto notably lacking in his character. Isaac is saved, but ironically in his cynical sense, not his father's pious one; the faked search gets Isaac enough money and fame to leave what he calls "the asshole of Tennessee" for New York and "success," his decidedly secular version of salvation. MacCarland Sumpter is a victim of disordered desires because he was late accepting the evil within his own heart and within his own son. Hell is prayer answered, desires fulfilled.

Similarly, Jeremiah Beaumont in *World Enough and Time* prepared his drama before learning of himself. Thus, deluded, he thinks he kills Cassius Fort, his friend and benefactor whose offense was to seduce Rachel before Jeremiah had even met her, as a sacrifice to his own self-determined abstract ideal of justice. But Warren tells us that the obligation to do murder really sprang from the dark depths of Jeremiah's nature. The reader is prepared to accept this assertion, for Jeremiah's blood lust has been well documented: his brooding from childhood on the picture of the female martyr being burned and his confusion over whether to imagine himself as rescuing her or as adding fuel to the fire, for example. Jeremiah does kill Fort; he gets what he asked for so earnestly and planned for so carefully, but guilt and despair ensue, not the blessed peace, certainty,

---

[3] Robert Penn Warren, *The Cave* (New York, 1959), p. 91. All subsequent references to *The Cave* are to this edition.

and definition he believed would be his. Not knowing himself, he chose Hell, not Heaven.

Yet another aspect of disordered desire deriving from a lack of self-knowledge is manifested in Warren's recurring victor-victim theme. Warren is fond of posing the questions: How innocent is innocence really? Does weakness invite plunder? Are we not all victors and victims both? In other words, Warren is speculating that the victim often merely gets what he wants. If the victim really knew his own heart, its evil, and his own secret desire to relinquish responsibility, to lay down the burden, would he not have to admit guilt as black, perhaps, as the despoilers? "Oh who is whose victim?" asks "poor," "innocent" Manty in *Band of Angels*. Her unprotected weakness invites her rape by Hamish Bond, and, later, she forces herself to admit that perhaps Bond was merely answering her secret and unuttered desire. Her reluctance was probably phony.

This theme is explored in great detail in *Brother to Dragons*. Lilburn Lewis horribly hacks to death, in the meathouse before the assembled slaves, the helpless George whose crime was to break a pitcher that had belonged to Lilburn's mother. But the worst of the affair is that Lilburn had planned his brutal atrocity *before* sending George to the spring with the pitcher. Surely it would seem that in this victor-victim relationship the evil is all on one side. But George wished to be hacked to death; he felt that his deed was a "peculiar fulfillment he has long lived with," and he wreaks "his merciless frailty" on Lilburn. Warren adds that George, like most victims, is a lover of "sweet injustice to himself."[4] Once again, the sin and the punishment, as in *The Inferno,* are identical.

Some of Warren's characters, however, desire and strive for the wrong things because of insufficient knowledge of the external world. The world is, Warren believes, enormously, almost overwhelmingly complex. Over and over he insists upon the necessity of knowledge of the world's complexity, even though all human knowledge must be partial. He has Jeremiah Beaumont conclude that knowledge is, after all, better than salvation or even peace, and R.P.W. in *Brother to Dragons* decides that all is redeemed in knowledge, "the bitter bread." The truth is deadly but it makes us free. With such a view, then, there can be no single keys to truth and certainty, no simple desires. Old Jebb in "Blackberry Winter" all his life had prayed for strength; now old, alone, like Tiresias he wants only

---

[4] Robert Penn Warren, *Brother to Dragons* (New York, 1953), p. 129. All subsequent references to *Brother to Dragons* are to this edition.

death. But his earlier prayers had been answered, and he is too strong to die. He tells the boy "A man doan know what to pray fer, and him mortal,"[5] and this bit of information provides perhaps the most significant element in the initiation of the narrator. So caught up in the clutter of events, many of Warren's characters fail to understand what old Jebb knows, that man's knowledge is rarely complete enough to know what he should want. Private Porsum in *At Heaven's Gate* recalls that in the heat of battle he had prayed to kill the twenty-two Germans manning the enemy bunker. He achieved his objective and became a hero, a role that brought him problems with which he cannot cope. Only too late, after being used by the financiers to exploit the mountaineers' admiration for him, does he realize that he should have made one more request — for the last bullet to hit him. Similarly, the shockingly ignorant baseball prodigy in "Goodwood Comes Back" got his one real desire — a farm of his own — by marrying a girl who owned one. He also got a brother-in-law with a twelve-gauge shotgun who shot him at point blank range in the kitchen one morning. Fulfillment, like desire, is never single and simple.

Band of Angels examines the larger, social implications of man's failure in knowledge and foresight. Tobias Sears, an Emersonian idealist, dedicated himself in the Civil War to fighting for two noble causes: saving the Union and freeing the slaves. But despite his and others' earnest actions he sees both these ideals betrayed in postwar America. The former slaves are handed over to the banks and made into chattels of the wage system, and the Union is so dedicated to rampant materialism and blatant commercialism that it has become "a league with dollars and a convenant with death."[6] Desired aims again were achieved, but because of deficient knowledge these aims, like those of the avaricious and prodigal in Dante's fourth circle, turn out to be exactly opposite to what was expected.

Man has at least some control over his disordered desires that yield unfortunate fulfillment: he can come to terms with his depraved nature and he can try to obtain knowledge that sometimes will save him, save him at least from a tragic naiveté and foolish idealism. But in Warren's cosmology one's desires are often tragically requited, not through any particular error or frailty, but rather because of the tragic nature of the world that sometimes taunts mankind by cruelly and ironically giving him his wishes. This is

---

[5] Robert Penn Warren, *The Circus in the Attic and Other Stories* (New York, 1947), p. 87. All references to short stories are to this edition.
[6] Robert Penn Warren, *Band of Angels* (New York, 1955). p. 343.

Warren's way of dramatizing Cass Mastern's idea that there is in life but one certainty: "damnation is ever at hand" (p. 177); life is fraught with peril for poor mankind lost in the deep and dark wood. As a device for structuring a plot this theme perhaps owes more to fairy tales than to Dante; it is the plot structure of such stories as "The Monkey's Paw" in which all wishes are granted but under conditions that negate their desirability.

In *At Heaven's Gate*, for instance, after the collapse of his world Jerry Calhoun returns to his father's old home, now fresh with all the improvements made by the Happy Valley Hunt Club, one of the failed enterprises of Bogan Murdock, the crooked speculator, the improvements Jerry had always wanted to make but never had. His wish was granted, but too late.

> He had wanted so many things and had had all of them and had had none of them, for what you had came wrong or too soon or too late, or it wore another face, and your three wishes always came true but the last undid all the rest, and you were where you had begun. (p. 387)

The world also tragically provides apt fulfillment to several other main characters in Warren's fiction. Willie Stark does get his wish — a hospital built free of graft. But in achieving his goal both he and his empire are destroyed. In the same novel Jack Burden gets his wish to avoid involvement when he refuses the naked and willing Anne with the weak rationalization that it would not be right. But by evading responsibility, by not committing himself to the future, he is actually forced into greater responsibility and guilt. Paolo and Francesca were doomed for all eternity for only once giving in to lust. By not succumbing Jack brings on the whole tragedy. He later reasons that if he had then taken Anne, his mother would have caught them; they then would have been married and Anne would never have become Willie's mistress, Jack never blackmailed Irwin, or Adam killed Willie. For Hamish Bond, too, fulfillment is tragically apt in *Band of Angels*. As a boy he left home because his ogreish mother degraded his father, mercilessly driving him to make more money. Leaving, Hamish promises her that he will get so rich that he will be "ass-deep in niggers." After Rau-Ru (a former slave whom Bond had loved and treated like a son) put the noose around his neck and after he sees Manty among the rioting freed slaves, Bond acts as his own executioner by jumping from the wagon into the mob. His last words are "ass-deep in niggers." Such a punishment for a slave trader would have appealed to Dante, who was also adept at making the punishment fit the crime.

Yet despite the tragic nature of the world, man can, in Warren's fiction, often achieve his desires without punishment. First are those usually weak characters who do what they intend in the deep recesses of the self, although they cannot admit even to themselves their real intention. While learning how to get ahead in the financial empire of Bogan Murdock, Jerry spent long evenings being tutored in economics by the brilliant Duckfoot Blake. As he began to find short-cuts to success — the right clothes, correct opinions, and, finally, the boss's daughter, he began to find reasons, always good and adequate, to pass up these sessions. Duckfoot, however, knew that we can usually do what we want: "I shore-God do think its miraculous how brute event can conform to the secret will of man," he tells the apologetic Jerry (p. 81). Similarly in *Flood* Dr. Calvin Fiddler breaks out of prison only to commit a deed that would insure his remaining forever in this refuge, the only place in the world where he really belongs. Like the shy and ineffectual Bolton Lovehart in "The Circus in the Attic," he had found his way back, out of history and the responsibility of time.

But there are also those characters who do what they intend by first overcoming the world, as much as is possible, and secondly by realistically modifying their intentions. Again like Dante, Warren testifies that men are responsible, rational beings. And both respect the limitations which the world and time force upon mankind. Hence in Warren no victory is ever complete, for his characters who succeed learn that they must work within the obstacles and frustrations inherent in the world and the human condition. That is, they must, like Jeremiah Beaumont, submit the dream to the world so that both the ideal and the real can fuse in a Hegelian synthesis. Adam Rosenzweig in *Wilderness* wins, but his is only a severely limited victory. In fact his story at first glance seems to be one of consistent defeat and frustration. In this chronicle of apparent failure Adam actually performs only one significant act: in the confusion of fleeing armies at the Battle of the Wilderness he kills a Rebel, more by chance than design. And, worse still, he admits that his shot was fired not on behalf of human freedom but out of weakness and error: he shot the Rebel because he himself was a cripple and the Rebel was not. This, then, is what the cruel irony of the world had prepared for Adam. By accepting his fate — the limitations of the world and the self — he is free to try to be worthy of what all men "in their error" must endure. So he did, after all, fire the shot for freedom but in a different and more limited sense than he had naively dreamed of doing. Hence, he realizes, *"We always do what we intend."*[7]

In both Dante and Warren this theme provides a philosophical irony at the very center of their chief concerns, not a mere structural contrivance. Thematically it provides the idea of peril and uncertainty for man. The path to the dark wood is ever at hand and the way to the mountain barred by wild beasts. Even with knowledge of the self and of the external world, man's position is not secure. It is precarious for the same kinds of reasons as Dante's world. Man is so sinful and ignorant that he rarely knows what to want, what to pray for. He must live with the awful knowledge that his prayers may be answered, his desires requited. With Dante there is a moral system inherent in the universe, the medieval Christian cosmology. With Warren, though, the risks are greater; there is more contingency in the universe, so much that a definite moral system cannot be deduced from its workings — witness the bitterly ironic "Confession of Brother Grimes" and the poem in which God, after sending a violent storm that destroys the poor farmer's corps, "got down on hands and knees/To peer and cackle and commend/His own sadistic idiocies."[8] In Warren's works desires are granted, it would seem, by blind chance working in the moil and clutter of events. But in Warren as in Dante men are responsible creatures. Warren's characters never reach a vision of God. The most they achieve is a limited glory. Adam hobbling out of the wilderness with his newly found truth, R.P.W. on the winter-shrunken mountain in Kentucky ready "To go into the world of action and liability," a world "Sweeter than hope in that confirmation of late light" (p. 215), a purged and chastened Bradwell Tolliver listening to the preacher's words, which he is too far away to hear distinctly, watching the slowly rising waters of the TVA lake flooding out his past — these epiphanies are to Warren comparable to Dante's beholding the white radiance of God.

---

[7] Robert Penn Warren, *Wilderness* (New York, 1961), p. 300.
[8] Robert Penn Warren, "Summer Storm (circa 1916) and God's Grace," in *Promises: Poems 1954-1956* (New York, 1957), p. 38.

2. Varied Critical Approaches

Robert Gorham Davis

Dr. Adam Stanton's Dilemma

In 1935, the year that Huey Long was shot and killed, Robert Penn Warren, a distinguished poet and associate professor at the University of Louisiana, began editing *The Southern Review* with Cleanth Brooks. It was one of the best and purest literary quarterlies in the United States, and it was paid for by a brilliant and unscrupulous vulgarian who had imposed a naked dictatorship of fraud and force on the State of Louisiana and who was now reaching out, through undercover alliances and Share-the-Wealth Clubs, for national power.

The Southern Review was completely free to print whatever its editors, men of integrity, thought best, and yet by that very fact, and by the presence of such men at the University of Louisiana, Long's ambitions were being served. He had poured millions of dollars into the university with a Fascist's love of buildings, particularly of stadiums. He had some of his happiest moments parading his heavily mechanized ROTC before visiting celebrities and personally conducting the huge bands and the elaborate cheering at football games. But his larger purpose was to win over the ambitious youth of the State and make them leaders in his national Share-the-Wealth program. Half the students at L.S.U. were getting money from State jobs, with all the corruption and intrigue inseparable from such an arrangement in Long's Louisiana.

Moreover, Huey Long interfered in university affairs in characteristic fashion. He forced the illegal award of a degree to a supporter in jail for obscene libel. He expelled honor students for criticizing his rule over student organizations. Such acts naturally aroused great protest. To forestall blacklisting by national educational organizations and to placate intellectuals, Long was shrewd enough to have able writers and teachers brought to the university and given freedom of expression and teaching as long as they let him have his way in politics.

The ethics of collaboration in such a regime, with medicine substituted for education, is the theme of *All the King's Men*. Should Dr. Adam Stanton, the aristocrat, the man of ideas, consent to run

Reprinted from *The New York Times Book Review*, 8 August, 1946, pp. 3, 24, by permission. Copyright © 1946 by *The New York Times*.

the great hospital built by the dictator, the man of action, Willie
Stark, whose methods he despises? Should his aloof pride keep him
out of living history just because it isn't as pure and objective
as science? Should a good man refuse to do greater good through
the aid of Willie Stark for fear some of Stark's dirt might stick to
the goodness?

Warren had been troubled by similar themes in his earlier fiction.
Night Rider, a historical novel of the organization of the tobacco
farmers, told what happened when violence was used as the last
resort in support of a just cause. His second novel, *At Heaven's Gate*,
was a dress rehearsal for *All the King's Men*. There, too, Warren
dealt with political and business corruption; with past and present
evil; with the relation of aristocrats and back countrymen. And he
used in part the story of a national figure, Sergeant Alvin York. But,
rich and complex though it was, *At Heaven's Gate* did not hold together. There was nothing to give it the unity, drive and immediacy
that the realities of Huey Long's career give *All the King's Men*.

For Robert Penn Warren is writing about the real Huey Long
even more frankly than Adria Locke Langley was in her very successful "A Lion Is in the Streets." The details of the hero's education, mannerisms and features; of the impeachment proceedings
and assassination, put this beyond question. The novel must be
judged, then, in political as well as literary terms, for its total effect
is to justify Long and the intellectuals who played ball with him; to
romanticize him; to have a kind of love affair with him through the
three women who adore him, one of them implausibly and inex-
plicably, the aristocratic heroine. The man of action and the man of
ideas yearn toward each other, "each incomplete with the terrible
division of their age." In between is the reporter Jack Burden, the
thoroughly unpleasant teller of the story, who is able to move freely
through the two worlds of ideas and action, of the new politics,
because he is nothing in himself.

It is not simply that Willie Stark is made to justify himself in
terms that Long might have used: that is, that a job had to be done
for the people of Louisiana, and was willing to play dirty politics if
that was necessary to get it done. "Dirt makes grass grow; a dia-
mond ain't a thing in the world but a piece of dirt that got awful hot.
And God-a-Mighty picked up a handful of dirt and blew on it and
made you and me and George Washington." But Warren also sim-
plifies and alters Long's career almost in the spirit of Parson Weems.
In an early scene in *All the King's Men*, the cynical reporter and
the fiery Irish girl secretary, like characters in a Clarence Budington

Kelland serial, get hold of the earnest young teetotaling politician who is the dupe of higher-ups and who is boring the people with theories and statistics. They tell him the truth, get him mad, get him drunk, and send him out to make the speech that launches his career. At the end of the novel, as a result of his son's paralysis in a football accident, Willie Stark reforms completely, goes back to his simple, good wife; breaks with his dishonest lieutenants, and tells the reporter with his dying breath that, if he had been spared, things would have been different from then on. The reporter becomes good, too. *All The King's Men*, is brilliantly done, with magnificent brief set-pieces in which Robert Penn Warren writes prose equivalent to his poems in sound and rhythm and imagery; lyric passages full of wisdom and acute observation about a boy's falling in love; about men growing old; about being a failure; about parents and children; about a cow seen at night; a woman seen from a train; friendships in childhood; changes of season in the slums. In his descriptive passages, Warren records almost too sharply, as if with glasses to overcorrect myopia, so that we stare from a few inches away at shreds of shuck lying in the pig's trough, or at the creping of a lovely woman's neck, or at japonica petals in a pool after rain, or at a man's cortex laid bare by the surgeon's knife.

Mixed with this pure gold is the brass of slick writing and melodrama that comprises the rest of the novel. Warren knows his trade. He has collaborated with Cleanth Brooks on a series of textbooks that have radically influenced the teaching of English in our best preparatory schools and colleges. But his writing can be false, nevertheless, as in the description of Anne Stanton, "that fine, slender, compactly made, tight-muscle, soft-fleshed, golden-shouldered mechanism," or of Burden's first wife, "a mystic combination of filet mignon and a Georgia peach, aching for the tongue and ready to bleed gold." And final drama is attained by extravagant use of Polti's famous thirty-six basic plot situations. Burden, for instance, causes the suicide of the man he did not know to be his father, and saves his mother's soul in doing it. Adam Stanton, later the assassin of Stark, operates on the spinal cord of the son of the man who had seduced his sister.

But it is the political pattern of "All the King's Men" that is really disturbing. The treatment of Negroes, always called "niggers" and given strictly Stephen Fetchit roles, is not surprising, since Warren contributed the piece, "The Briar Patch," to the Southern manifesto, "I'll Take My Stand," and had written earlier a whole book attacking the legend of John Brown. It is not surprising that he should assume that Long's program would economically benefit the mass of the people, despite evidence to show that, through squandering money, lowering wage rates and imposing indirect or hidden taxes, Long made their situation worse. But it is surprising that *All the King's Men* never really faces the threat of men like Long to the democratic process itself.

Robert Penn Warren is fascinated by the strong man of action, as many of our war novelists were fascinated by romanticized Nazis. And the question of *All the King's Men* is solely whether the man of ideas can work with the dictator in the interests of historic change; whether, in carrying out that change, the unscrupulous vulgarian is not really a better man than the selfish, dignified, discreet and also immoral politicians from whom he seized power. Warren does not ask — the question apparently has no imaginative appeal for him — whether American tradition does not demand that we fight men like Long with the utmost resolution and with all the democratic means at our disposal, in order to preserve in this country and in the world free, open, pluralistic societies in which individual rights are protected by law and in which ultimate control is invested below in the people and not above in Willie Stark. Anyone able to swallow the dictator's tempting logic of *All the King's Men* will find an instant emetic in a few random savorings of the real Huey Long as described by such reporters as Forrest Davis, Carleton Beals and Harnett T. Kane.

Charles R. Anderson

Violence and Order in the Novels of Robert Penn Warren

The works of major authors often have a unity that tempts the critic to look for a central theme, even a controlling symbol, that focuses their vision of life. I find all the novels of Robert Penn

Reprinted from *Southern Renascence: The Literature of the Modern South*, Louis D. Rubin, Jr. and Robert D. Jacobs, eds. (Baltimore: The Johns Hopkins Press, 1953), pp. 207-25, by permission of the publisher. Copyright © 1953 by the John Hopkins Press.

Warren to be variations on a single theme, symbolized in the polarities of violence and order. He could not have chosen two concepts more arresting to the modern reader or more deeply embedded in the history of his country and his region.

American history began with a tremendous uprooting from settled European cultures because of uncompromising religious dissent and economic restlessness. The first century and a half was a continuous chronicle of international rivalries, Indian wars, and struggles for survival against a hostile environment — threatened famine, extremes of climate, wild beasts and savages. Then came the violence of revolt from the mother country, with the doctrine of continuous revolution announced as an inalienable right, followed in less than a century by a bloody Civil War. And all along, just beyond the settlements, there was always the frontier with the original conditions of violence repeated in wave after wave across the continent until the end of the nineteenth century. The smooth surface of contemporary life in this country does not conceal from the poet the same patterns reappearing today in the ruthless drive of big business and power politics, as well as in the more obvious orgies of speed, prohibition, race riots, and gangsters.

Robert Penn Warren has uncovered the historical sources of American violence and made them available for literary purposes, all four novels taking off from violent episodes in history that are used to illuminate modern meanings. But in writing tragedy, though the downward plunge into action takes up the most space and provides the greatest interest, violence alone is not enough. The tragic note cannot be struck without a positive world view. There can be no fall unless there is something to fall from; disorder is meaningless without order, at least a concept of order, as a point to measure from. Hemingway's fiction is an instructive example. He writes of violence in a world of violence, even the milieu being carefully placed outside the ordered daily life of man. Though each of his heroes has a sort of code to live by — that of the soldier, the sportsman, even the criminal — it is not a discipline applicable to the normal world. This is perhaps best illustrated by bull-fighting, where the violence of the bull is contrived and the code of fighting him is entirely artificial. It is aesthetically pure, like a problem in geometry, and hence devoid of moral meaning. It is not tragedy. In Warren's fictions, though violence predominates at least on the surface, a concept of order is always there as a touchstone; and since the source of both is to be found in his Southern heritage, this may explain why Warren (and Faulkner) alone of modern American novelists can write tragedies.

Collective myth has fixed on the South as the embodiment of violence in America. The witch-burning of New England, the bandit of the Wild West, the underworld of Chicago, all of them fade before the succession of Southern images of violence that fascinate the popular mind: the lash of the slave-driver, the Bowie knife of the old Southwest, the duelling pistol of the hot-headed gentleman, the rebel yell of the fire-eater, the gasoline torch of the lyncher, the fiery cross of the Klansman. One can indeed point to certain historical factors that made for greater potential violence in the South. By reason of its geographical shape as a fringe of seaboard states, this region was more continuously exposed to the frontier than other more compact areas of settlement. With a third of its population only a few generations out of African savagery, there was always the fact of primitive behavior as well as the threat of slave insurrection. The plantation system made the enforcement of discipline and the democratization of culture harder than in the more populous townships of the North, so that the poor-whites tended to sink into lawlessness instead of being educated into good citizenship. When the power of the ruling class was smashed, the incidence of violence in the post-bellum South rose above that of the rest of the nation, as the recent statistics of a criminologist have proved.

However interesting all this may be to the historian and sociologist, it merely provides a subject matter — not a theme — for the novelist like Warren who is concerned with something quite different from the game of cops and robbers. He is concerned with moral order and moral violence, which sometimes coincide with physical order and violence in the world of men yet sometimes seem strangely to clash with them. So for the fictional artist, who must embody his theme in society, there are opened up rich possibilities of ambiguity and irony. For Warren murder, rape, and arson are simply the most effective dramatic means of developing one half his theme: that *violence is life without principle.* Nor, to illustrate the other half, does he use orderliness for its own sake (there are no police chiefs or private detectives among his heroes); to him *order is living by principles,* even when the particular effort to do so falls far short of perfection. Yet sometimes the man of principles also may be forced into violent action to defend or reassert a concept of order, when corrupt or misguided men have risen to power and society has lost its moorings. Again, external order on the political and economic levels may all too frequently be achieved, at least temporarily, by the kind of compromise which is a "deal" based on the abdication of principles. By such conflicts of appearances and realities Warren renders in his fictions the ambiguities of the actual world, as opposed to the blacks and whites of an imaginary one.

A further irony is woven into his stories by discriminating the man of principles from the idealist, with whom he is popularly confused. Without attempting to fix the final meaning of that vexed word, *principles*, one may begin with the dictionary definition: "the general or accepted laws governing conduct" that have come down through history. Quite opposite are those flights of the spirit enjoining us that we should love our neighbors as ourselves, that all men are created equal; these are aspirations, not principles. So with the humanitarianism of the abolitionist, the absolutism of the Puritan dogma of man's depravity, as well as the transcendental insistence on his divinity. Such are the so-called "principles" that frequently lead to extreme and even violent action, to the over-throw of the existing order in a search for Utopia; they are, instead, abstract ideals born of man's pride in his reason or of spiritual naiveté. At certain crises in the world's history, when stagnant traditionalism has retarded overdue reform, anarchic idealists play a legitimate role. Only after they have announced their extremist doctrines is it possible to take the middle of the road. Then the man of principles, accepting the mixture of good and evil in his nature, can take account of the new ideas as well as the traditional codes of morality drawn from human experience and re-establish an ordered society.

This is, at least, what Poe meant by principles and what Twelve Southerners took their stand on in 1930: man must accept his middle place in "nature" between the animals and the angels, neither sinking into naturalism nor aspiring to perfection, but creating the best possible order out of his recognized limitations and preserving it. It is chiefly, I suspect, what gives continuity to the literary tradition in the South (as distinctive as that in New England), from the pragmatic humanism of William Byrd to Faulkner's concern with "the old universal truths" that lie at the heart of his fictions, as summed up in his Nobel Prize speech. At any rate, the sociologists who have been appalled by Southern violence in the physical world have overlooked an equally high incidence of Southern concern with the principles of order, in the literary theory of Poe and Lanier as well as in the social and political theory of Jefferson and Calhoun, a tradition that has flowered anew in the agrarian poets and critics of the twentieth century. (It is precisely those elements of idealism based on abstract reason in Jefferson's philosophy that have been rejected in the South.)

The civilization of the South was founded on the concept of an ordered society. The basis for this is probably agrarianism, predicated on the European philosophy of a settled order, as opposed to industrialism, predicated on a belief in progress — with the necessary corollary of a changing way of life, however orderly the process.

The South has always distrusted progressivism and all the other isms that seem disruptive to a traditional society, a clearly defined order of human existence. That is, until the twentieth century, when cracks in this conservative civilization begin to show as the South, more and more industrialized, tends to lose its identity and become gradually transformed into the money economy of standardized urban America. It is a sense of this breaking-up as tragic that has focused the vision of the new Southern writers, who call back images of an older order — that they find better because more human — to measure the collapse into the political and moral chaos of the modern world. Warren's values are not founded on any theory of politics, economics, or religion, however, though most of his illustrative action takes place in these areas. He is a psychologist and a moralist, concerned with a particular conception of human nature (as Irene Hendry has pointed out, *Sewanee Review*, January 1945): Man cannot live in the world without a center of self-knowledge; hence the archetypal hero is the man with a full and immediate awareness of the fundamental principles according to which one acts in any given situation. Warren's concepts of violence and order are defined in Southern terms. Being a true artist, he does not argue these concepts nor use the terms explicitly in his novels; rather, he implies them in his symbolism, he renders them in the speech and behavior of his characters. Principles are embattled equally by corrupt materialism and by abstract idealism.

His first novel, *Night Rider* (1939), is set in the Kentucky Tobacco War of 1904. The association of farmers, organized for protection against the buyers' monopoly, at first seems based on principles. Some of the founders are high-minded, and there is much righteous indignation about unfair prices, much talk of justice and order. But unable to get justice fast enough by orderly methods, they set up the "night riders" to coerce reluctant farmers to join the association by scraping their plant beds, and even by burning barns and horsewhipping their owners. For a while the leaders managed to keep a sort of military discipline; but they have substituted force for principles — armed men operating in masks — and violence soon takes over. Recalcitrant members are shot down in cold blood by their fellow "klansmen"; mobs a thousand strong march on the towns and engage in mass arson, dynamiting the warehouses of the tobacco trust. A virtual war is precipitated, of such violence that the state militia has difficulty in restoring order. The background handling of this historical episode is almost documentary, but the center of interest in the novel lies elsewhere.

The author merely uses the tobacco war to illustrate the fall of Percy Munn from a sense of order to a fascination with violence for its own sake. His daemonic flaw is clarified by comparison with several other characters. The nearest to an idealist in this story is the combination of theory and practice represented by Professor Ball and his son-in-law Dr. MacDonald, who organize the night riders. They are determined men who produce effective action; they have noble convictions about justice but their abstract ideals of human behavior bear little relation to human experience, so that their goals can be achieved only by the ruthless application of force. They are not bad in the sense of being corrupt, but because their fanaticism does not recognize human limitations — a different kind of evil from that of pure materialism (which is represented, ironically, by a family named Christian). Further along in self-knowledge is the peasant Willie Proudfit, whose adventures in the far West and the religious conversion that brings him back to primitive agrarianism in Kentucky are told in an embedded story. Although these experiences do not furnish him with any articulate "ideals" about life, his rebirth gives him a sort of center from which to live — a not altogether successful embodiment of the regionalist theme of the small farmer who has returned "home."

The ambiguity of appearances is best brought out in two contrasting leaders of the association whose example led Munn to join. Only Captain Todd, whose character sets the moral tone of the early meetings, always acts on principles. But when he withdraws in protest at the formation of the night riders, Munn is too deeply involved in the excitement to follow him, rationalizing that he is just a Confederate veteran too old-fashioned to be effective in public affairs any longer. Instead, his eye is caught by the shining figure of Senator Tolliver, whose suave manners and eloquence in behalf of the oppressed farmers strike him as the qualities of a true leader who knows his direction. The reader from the beginning doubts his sincerity and gradually suspects him of being a confused and fragmentary man who must fulfill himself in other people, whose craving for applause and prestige may well lead to opportunism. But the hero does not recognize him as the hollow man he is until he sells out to the trust, a man of price rather than principle. (It is apparent now that Tolliver joined the association in the first place for political advantage, just as he resigned and secretly went over to the enemy for a greater advantage.) By this time Munn, from a promising young lawyer aspiring to an ordered life, has sunk to an anonymous group-murderer and a fugitive from justice. The completeness of his disintegration is revealed by his final resolve to murder the Senator, whom he at last sees as a moral negation ("You were always nothing," he tells him); but he lacks the will to carry out even this, and in the night he is riddled with bullets by the posse sent to capture him. Such is the tragedy of Percy Munn, who lacked the ability to formulate a set of principles adequate to conduct, or even to recognize them in the noble example of Captain Todd whom he admired and who, at least for the reader, is a point from which to measure the hero's fall into violent and suicidal action.

Warren's second novel, *At Heaven's Gate* (1943), is based on the actual career of Luke Lea, who built up a precarious financial kingdom in Tennessee through ruthless business methods and political corruption and was criminally prosecuted for his part in a multi-million-dollar failure in the crash of 1929. But the financier Bogan Murdock could never have been a protagonist to Warren, as the titan Cowperwood was to Dreiser. For, wholly given over to a blind drive for economic power — modern "civilized" violence — he has no principles from which to fall. He cannot be a center of interest but only a point of reference, and a device for irony. Murdock is the sham man-of-principles, heightened and extended from the Senator of the first novel. Outwardly he is an accomplished man of the world, a perfect host unfailingly courteous, impeccable in speech and behavior. His apparent mastery of life is symbolized in his mastery of a horse, his flashing equestrianism seeming the final flourish of the eighteenth-century gentleman. It is only gradually that the reader realizes the moral vacuum beneath this polished surface. It is his economic adviser Blake who first sees that he is empty inside ("When Bogan looks in the mirror he don't see a thing," says the cynical Ph.D.). Order, we learn, is not the same thing as decorum, though this may be the form in which it clothes itself. Order is living by principles, and Murdock has given them up in his abstract passion for financial power; he is as ruthless in this as men of an earlier day had been in action. This not only brings us nearer to the contemporary world, but it proves that moral violence is more destructive than physical violence, because it results from the corruption of principles and produces a continuing state of chaos rather than a temporary one.

Most of the evil in this novel operates under cover of big business or respectable society, and the center of interest radiates out to the circle of characters surrounding Murdock. The first inkling of disorder is the discovery that he has no control over his own family. His senile father, whose past murder of a political rival Bogan is covering up, is threatening at all points to blurt out the secret; his neglected wife is an alcoholic; his daughter is a nymphomaniac. Sue and Murdock's protégé Jerry, the Phi Beta Kappa football hero, unconsciously feel the emptiness of their lives attached to this man of no principles; they indulge in violent and joyless copulation in an unhappy effort to find their identity in each other, then break off their engagement and lose all direction as they throw their weight around generally. Physical violence, which has been kept off-stage in flashbacks and embedded stories, is saved for the denouement where it is piled on too thick to be disentangled here. Among the minor figures there are plenty of grubby materialists hanging on Murdock's coat-tails ready to use physical force if necessary to cash in on the potentialities for corruption in his interlocking system, but as the epitome of modern moral violence the boss is careful to maintain appearances. As a result, most of the external violence is deflected from him to his daughter and her fiancé. Sue, in her desperate flight from her father's emptiness and Jerry's confusion, has gone to live with a drunken chaotic group of Bohemians. She has an abortion performed because one of them, a Marxian bruiser, refuses to marry her; she is strangled by another, a homosexual, in impotent rage; the family's negro butler is nearly lynched for her murder; and Jerry lands in jail as the scapegoat for Murdock's financial collapse.

In this complex novel the emphasis is so distributed among a large gallery of characters, most of whom suffer in various stages from the modern disease of "division," that any attempt to summarize their meanings must be tentative. There are several partial manifestations of the idealist. Blake, who gives Jerry worldly advice on how to achieve financial eminence, is an inverted one, as proved by his cynicism and his sentimental discovery in the end that some things really matter. The most fully developed idealist is Sweetwater, a preacher's son who ran away from home to become a strike-promoter for the unions, and who has managed to define himself through identification with the abstract cause of the working man. But he is not a man of principles. He can only find direction from the outside, from the Marxist's code, a partial one invented by man's reason to right an economic wrong; and he carries over this code to his love affair with Sue, rejecting the human relation of marriage because it would interfere with his dedication. (The inner discipline of the man of principles aims at a whole view, self imposed by reference to the orders of religion and traditional society against which imperfect man can be measured.) If Sweetwater fails in wholeness because he is dominated by reason, the opposite is true of Wyndham, the fanatic of the interpolated story, though his primitive religion at least provides him with an adequate understanding of evil; but both men lack balance and are led into violence by their idealism. The most vivid symbol of the divided man is the sexual ambivalence of Slim Sarrett, the intellectual who oscillates between pugilism and poetry, between a tendency to homosexuality and a desire to have Sue as his mistress. It is dramatically fitting that she should come to a violent end at his hands, for she is as incapable of finding a center from which to live as he (or as Percy Munn). The bewildered Jerry Calhoun, like all the others, is a divided modern man, but he alone finds a measure of redemption. In his bumbling, persistent way he finally recognizes Murdock as an a-moral monster in time to save himself from contamination and makes a symbolic return to his humble home and father (the favorite pattern of all Warren's "Billy Pottses"). But neither he nor old man Calhoun, the simple, clumsy dirt-farmer, is strong enough to serve convincingly as the exemplary man of principles. At best, this almost naturalistic novel is a study in the disintegration of modern society, the confusion of man lost in the disorder of his blindly competitive urban economy and trying to find some truth by which to live. But it falls short of tragedy; there is no cruel defeat through excess of virtue. And since the hero who acts on principles does not appear except in shreds and patches, there is no standard from which a fall can be measured.

All the King's Men (1946), first drafted as a play, is his fullest achievement of tragedy. Though it follows in some detail the outward career of Huey Long, dictator of Louisiana from 1928 until his assassination in 1935, it was not Warren's purpose to write a fictional biography of the King Fish. By the device of the narrator he frames one story within another, so that the rise and fall of Willie Stark become merely illustrative matter. Though this master of violence is the one who comes to a tragic end, the reader's interest centers in Jack Burden, the rootless and alienated modern man, a symbol of the "terrible division of his age" that makes a Stark possible. He alternately withdraws as a spectator to formulate a theory of life and swings back into action to reform the world (at least by proxy); but he continues his search for self-knowledge which, in the end, saves him from physical catastrophe.

In his first novel Warren had effectively used "night" as a symbol of the darkness in which men move. In his ironically titled *At Heaven's Gate*, the representative image seems to be "pus," the evil being now clearly in the blood-stream, a part of man's essential nature and not an external thing that can be eliminated automatically by reform and progress. So in *All the King's Men* essential evil is internal, chiefly expressed in terms of political corruption. And the outward manifestations of order are again ironical symbols.[1] The network of paved highways Stark builds over the state, with Route 58 forming a sort of structural spine for the novel, is to be the pattern of his new order of prosperity. But they are never shown to be paths of direction: nobody knows where he is going in this book, so the roads lead everywhere and nowhere. Instead of economic aids to the common man, they chiefly produce speed and meaningless action, or bring the wool-hat boys pouring into the capital to chant like primitives, "We want Willie!" It is from an accident on one of these shining concrete strips that Tom Stark, rebelling against the domination of his action-mad father, receives his basic injury. The second instrument of the new order Stark had promised the people was education, but his emphasis is on football, with its artificial discipline mimicked in the parades of bands and organized cheering. It is his forcing Tom into a game when not in condition — anything to win — that results in the final injury. This leads to Willie's third panacea, free medical care. But the only use we hear of the hospital being put to — besides an operation to restore a schizophrenic to singleness — is Dr. Stanton's effort to save Tom. Science, alas, cannot make him whole again, and action for its own sake ends in paralysis. Order, we learn through tragic irony, cannot be imposed mechanically from the outside.

Stark's new order can only lead to destructive violence because he plunges headlong into action with no clearly defined principles. In

---

[1] Norman Girault, the only critic who has noted the contrasted symbolism of violence and order in this novel, has already pointed out two examples (see *Accent*, Summer 1947). The stagnant water covered with algae that surrounds the little islands of civilization in Louisiana Warren describes as "the bayou, which coiled under the moss ... heavy with the hint and odor of swamp, jungle, and darkness, along the edge of the expanse of clipped lawn" — a juxtaposition of uncontrollable brute nature and man's rationally controlled efforts to stake out a claim. Closely connected with this is a second symbol, Highway 58, and the novel opens significantly with the dare-devil driving of SugarBoy down this new road cut through the swamp. Even nature seems to resent this, as it does Stark's blind drive for power, "the ectoplasmic fingers of the mist" reaching out to snag the roaring Cadillac; but the dictator's body-guard shows his pride in the mastery of machinery, and his hatred of nature, by deliberately swerving to run down a snake. Warren seems to be saying that modern man's attempt to control the external world through the orderly will, unguided by an understanding of irrational violence, is not the way to the good life.

his drive for power he becomes an opportunist who makes deals, and is soon entangled in a mesh of bribery and graft demanding coercive measures to hold his empire of outlaws in check. The air is charged with potential violence as the police state takes shape: the bullet-proof limousine, the body-guard Sugar Boy practising fast draws with his .38, the natty élite State Patrol, the threat of illiterate mobs. But during three-fourths of the book it occurs only in the embedded story of Cass Mastern, whose history Jack was trying to make a doctoral dissertation but was stopped because unable to read the meaning of violence and order in his ancestor's life. This lesson is learned in a bath of blood as the novel roars to its end. Judge Irwin resigns from his post at Attorney General because he can no longer stomach the dictator's methods,* then commits suicide when confronted by Stark with the dirt from his past previously dug up by Jack; and Jack learns too late, from his mother's confession, that he has unwittingly killed his father. Anne Stanton, whose world of ordered values is shattered by discovering that her father had been implicated in the Judge's guilt, breaks her engagement with Jack and throws herself into the arms of Stark, the one man in all this chaos who seems to have strength and direction. This brings on the climax. For her idealist brother, Dr. Adam Stanton, who learns of her dishonor through the jealousy of Stark's rejected mistress Sadie Burke and the welching of Tiny Duffy, assassinates the dictator under the dome of the capitol. Sugar Boy pumps him full of lead from his automatic, the squealer Tiny narrowly misses a like fate, and Sadie collapses in a mental hospital. So the bodies pile up in the tradition of Elizabethan tragedy, and only Jack and Anne are left to find their way back to a meaningful life.

The ambiguities of real life are reproduced so faithfully in this fiction that all Warren's characters become people instead of types, but it may help clarify his meanings to look for the main springs of his creative thinking. The foreground is crowded with corrupt materialists — almost all the king's men. There is his machine organization of political henchmen, most fully delineated in the predatory Duffy; and there is a whole implied ring of unscrupulous capitalists who finance his reforms for a cut or a monopoly. The brute materialism of some of those closest to him is slightly humanized by being based on blind love and devotion to the dictator instead of selfish

---

*Editor's note. Actually it is not Judge Irwin but Hugh Miller who served for a time as Attorney General under Governor Stark and then resigned out of disgust with some of Stark's methods.

greed, as with the moronic Sugar Boy and the carnal Sadie. The wool-hat boys whose suffrage supports him are only materialists in the sense of having never been sure of a square meal; hence their fanatic loyalty to Willie, because of their naive trust in his promises. It is not implied that they are corrupt, but they are capable of mass violence if it is needed to keep him in the saddle. Stark himself is not a pure materialist, for he is far less concerned with any tangible "take" for himself than with a mania for abstract power. This of course is largely motivated by selfish passions: ambition, the drive to compensate for being born a "have-not," and revenge against the politicos who duped him at the beginning of his career. But it is also curiously mixed with an initial idealism, to redeem government and give it back to the people, threads of which keep reappearing. He is constantly trying to persuade himself that his purpose is to bring good out of evil, and he makes at least one striking attempt to put his power at the service of a humanitarian ideal by excluding the politicians from influence in the medical center where Dr. Stanton is at the helm. None of this, however, must be confused with principles. A man of principles is above all one who can understand and control himself, and this is precisely what Willie cannot do, though he can face and manage everything and everybody else. His genius is for action, without waiting to formulate principles; in the material world this leads to opportunism, pyramiding violence, and final destruction.

Warren is just as critical of the idealist as he is of the materialist, and there are several of them here to complicate the issues. Jack Burden's supposed father is a pious fool who deserts his wife and withdraws from the world into an impossible religion, trying to live out quite literally in the slums the gospel of Christ. (Warren may find the Christian scheme of things close to the facts of experience, as one critic suggests, but he is too much of an empiricist to trust the adequacy of an idealized Christianity to cope with the chaos of contemporary life.) His fiancée, Anne Stanton, is likewise a sheltered idealist who has never outgrown the innocence of childhood and is equally helpless in finding direction for herself or poor confused Jack. Her brother Adam is another case of withdrawal, too purely a man of ideas, who spurns the world of men for the truth of science (the emphasis on the abstraction of scientism is even stronger in the stage version, with its continuous chorus of surgeons chanting doggerel). His one venture into action is almost ritualistic, though by it he rid the state of a dictator. Yet one feels that all of this group — remnants of a traditional society — had drifted into their various idealisms because the codified principles of their civilization had become too formal and functionless, and because these characters were not secure enough in self-knowledge to dare acquire that knowledge of the modern world necessary to bring them into effective action. In a happier day they could have served, even though passively, as supporters of a way of life based on principles.

Even Jack Burden has this same tendency towards idealism, or its reverse, a wise-cracking cynicism, which keeps him wavering throughout most of the story from one half-truth to another. But he has a strong sense of social obligation and is too courageous a seeker to be content with so negative a life, and in the end his tragic experience of life makes possible his rebirth. From all he has learned, he defines his perfect exemplar as the man who has a body of principles which both initiate and control his actions, a balance resulting from knowledge of the world and moral certainty of self. Warren is too much of a realist to set up such a paragon in any single character, but from all the people at Burden's Landing one can be pieced together. Judge Irwin, the hero's real father, though a gentleman of the old school, was still capable of functioning effectively in public affairs; and he always acted on principles except for one slip in early life, but his failure to face the consequences of this resulted in his suicide. Cass Mastern, his great uncle from the previous century, died a hero (at least in the religious sense) because he acknowledged his evil for what it was and lived with it, never violating principles thereafter. From these imperfect examples Jack can construct his model. He can now accept the responsibility of being human, face the evil in the world and his part in it. He can find the faith and courage to give up his role of narrator and go back "into the convulsion of the world" — the contemporary world, which includes cities and science, political machines as well as industrial ones.

Warren's latest novel, *World Enough and Time* (1950), is an epitome of all that has gone before, but the author gives himself new dimensions by completely breaking with realistic fiction. He adopts melodrama as his subject matter and allegory as his vehicle, but shoulders them both off onto the "diary" kept by his hero. The foundation of his story is the famous "Kentucky Tragedy," a murder that took place in Frankfort in 1826 and has come down in elaborate documentary records. Though Jeremiah Beaumont of the novel goes through many of the acts of the original murderer, the theme is again the tragic search for order in a world of violence. As the hero says (though the documents are silent): "The idea by which a man would live gets lost in the jostle and pudder of things."

The vivid background of violence in early Kentucky, when civilization was just raising its head in the wilderness, is epitomized near the beginning in the description of a frontier revivalist:

> He belonged to that old race of Devil-breakers who were a terror and a blessing across the land, men who had been born to be the stomp-and-gouge bully of a tavern, the Indian fighter with warm scalps at his belt, the ice-eyed tubercular duelist of a country courthouse, the half-horse, half-alligator abomination of a keelboat, or a raper of women by the cow pen, but who got their hot prides and cold lusts short-circuited into obsessed hosannas and a ferocious striving for God's sake.

This summary is profusely illustrated throughout the novel, culminating in a carnival of violence in the embedded story of "la Grand' Bosse." He is a humpbacked pirate who rules over his kingdom of outlaws on an island in the swamp, where they wallow in filth and obscenity, liquor and lechery, ignorance and brawling, renegades of mixed blood and creeds. From this retreat they conduct raids on the Mississippi River traffic, murdering, burning, and bringing back the plunder of civilization to their primitive village built on stilts over the mud flats. This we are told, with an irony that undercuts the ideal of the primitivists, is "the innocence of nature." Man, it is clear, should not live according to Nature, but according to the principles of human nature.

The most significant violence, of course, is that in which the hero is involved as a major participant. With a romantic gesture Jerry breaks off his legal apprenticeship to Cassius Fort, whom he had looked up to as the ideal statesman, and seeks out in marriage a society belle whom Fort has seduced. For a while he tries to live with her in retirement from the world. But feeling a compulsion that her honor must be avenged he issues a challenge. When Fort, though admitting his guilt, refuses to duel his "adopted son," Jerry murders him in cold blood. At his trial he is very nearly acquitted through a web of shrewd lies, but is finally convicted by an even more intricate one. Condemned to be hanged, he is joined in the cell by his previously estranged wife. In a parody of rediscovered love they indulge in an orgy of sexual intercourse; failing to find escape in life they seek one in death, but the suicide pact fails to come off — the laudanum contained an emetic. That same night, just before the hour of their execution, they are rescued in a hairbreadth jail-delivery and taken to the island of la Grand' Bosse as a hideout. Here Jerry gradually sinks into that life of violence, while his wife loses her mind and kills herself with a hunting knife. A final prick of conscience sends him back to civilization to give himself up to the hangman and find expiation in facing his own guilt at last. But he is overtaken on the way by a hired assassin, decapitated, and only his head is brought back to justice. So much for the melodrama in which the violence is manifested.

This sensational sequence of events on the frontier reproduces convincingly the violent growth from which modern America has come, but in summary it reduces the novel unjustly to a tale of blood and thunder. Further, though the surface action may seem obvious, the meanings Warren draws from it are not. For example, to assume that America has progressed to better times by policing all this physical violence into law and order is to be brought up short with the implications of the end of la Grand' Bosse's career. It is the advance of "civilization" itself, we are told, that put the river pirate out of business, by inventing methods of making profits too subtle and complicated for him to understand or cope with: "He was simply the victim of technological unemployment." And we are not spared the ironical conjecture that some of his bastard descendants, masquerading in the world as respectable leaders and business men, "still carry under their pink scrubbed hides and double-breasted sack suits . . . the mire-thick blood of his veins and the old coiling darkness of his heart" — thus linking this pioneer incarnation of evil with the Bogan Murdocks and the Tiny Duffys of his modern fictions. Warren always makes it clear that he is concerned with the unchanging nature of man rather than with the changing social fabric in which this nature manifests itself. He chooses a particular time and place merely because of its illustrative value; and the profuse display of physical violence in early Kentucky makes vividly dramatic Jerry Beaumont's struggle towards a concept of order.

The author's meanings are made most explicit by the allegorical cast of the hero's mind, as he spells out the events and characters of his story in a diary. But one cannot always be certain of them because of his excessive ambition to corner the ultimate truth; for the defect of this novel lies in too many unresolved ambiguities, the failure to clarify some of its immensely complex significances. In a sense all the characters in *World Enough and Time* are projections of various aspects of the narrator (in the opening chapter the whole story is spoken of as "the drama Jeremiah Beaumont devised"); and his interpretations of them, recorded in a deliberately unrealistic style, tend to the abstractions of allegory. Two of them, his best friend and his wife, are clearly *alter egos* who give new definitions to the polarities of violence and order. Wilkie Barron is the purest

Man of Action in all Warren's fiction, too engrossed in the act of living to be concerned with its meanings; if he ever attempts to express an idea it becomes rhetoric, and he laughs at his own mock eloquence. He is the instigator of every action the hero takes part in — his marriage, his political brawling with the reformers, his mud-slinging campaign for the legislature, his murder of Colonel Fort. In the end Jerry recognizes him as at once his adversary and his shadow, calling him specifically "the mask of all the world." Rachel Jordan, the injured heroine "immured in an autumn world" of poetry, is the symbol of his dreaming; and he tries to escape with her into the inner secret world of love and honor, in a house from which the public is quite literally locked out. At the peak of their romance they are described as "high allegorical figures acting out their ritual." Standing midway between them is Skrogg, the newspaper editor who lashes the Relief Party into violent action to secure justice for the downtrodden. He is a fearless idealist, we are told, "because the world outside himself was not real, . . . was nothing but chaos which could become real only in so far as it was formed by his idea." Lest there be any doubt about the author's attitude towards this purest Man of Idea, his career after the reform movement failed is sketched in brief: by a fantastic reversal he entered the world he had scorned, became a professional duelist who killed half-a-dozen men, and was finally shot down by a man he had defamed.

As Jerry is drawn alternately to order (which in his idealism he defines as "the idea of the world") and violence ("the world itself"), he finds both inadequate and cries out for singleness, for some truth by which a man can live. In his search for principles he has many partial teachers. The first is Dr. Burnham of the classical academy, scholar, physician, and loving preacher, who holds up to him the example of the noble Romans; his second is Colonel Fort, the intelligent man of action, who tries to do what good he can in public affairs within his limitations, and takes Jerry on as a protégé. They are not perfect men, not even great men save that "they took their world greatly . . . and knew that in study, field, and forum they bore the destiny of men." But the youthful hero, in his obsession with perfection and certainty, drifts away from one and turns his dagger against the other. (In his effort to provoke Fort to a duel he tries to unite his inner and outer worlds, seeking in that code the formalized public act that embodies the idea of honor, but he is refused this ritualistic evasion. Condemned to death he tries to blame his botched life on Burnham for setting him impossible ideals, but his older teacher's last heroic act of goodness closes that escape from responsibility.) In the end Jerry's idealism, which has rejected the limitations of humanity and spurned the demands of society, humbles him enough to admire once more man's struggle to live by principles. The two lawyer-statesmen who volunteer to defend him at the murder trial provide him with a composite example: Hawgood, who lived selflessly for a high concept of truth, and Madison, a more experienced man, who felt honor bound to help all those suffering from injustice. For that one moment "the seasoned campaigner and the Platonic student" stood together, "worldly decency conspired with unworldly truth."

Jerry's life has partaken in some degree of all these, chiefly fluctuating between the extremes of idealism and materialism, in his search for a center. As he sifts for the meaning of his tumultuous and tragic experiences, he records his three great errors. The first was his withdrawal into "cold exile from mankind" believing that "the idea was all." The second was, "when we find that the idea has not redeemed the world, the world must redeem the idea" — which led to the confusion of means with end. The third error was "to deny the idea and its loneliness and embrace the world as all," to try to live in the innocence of nature. These had been the ways of his tragic life. His conclusion must be quoted in full:

> There must be a way I have missed. There must be a way whereby the world becomes flesh. There must be a way whereby the flesh becomes word. Whereby loneliness becomes communion without contamination. Whereby contamination becomes purity without exile. There must be a way; but I may not have it now. All I can have now is knowledge.

His diary ends with a question, the age-old human question, "Was all for naught?" But Warren's four novels, if we probe beneath the living tissue of the text, help to define Jerry's conclusion: Man must live *in* the world of violence, *by* whatever principles of order he can formulate and believe in. The man who makes up personal rules as expediency dictates or abstract ideals based on imperfect knowledge of the world falls into violence, moral or physical, almost as surely as the materialist who denies the validity of morals in a naturalistic universe. They all act against, not with, the ethical currents of their society. A didactic novelist unconcerned with tragedy might well have opposed to them the formalist, who rigidly adheres to the accepted civil and religious codes; but he can only function as a preserver of law and order in an established society. Instead, the heroic figure in these fictions is the man of principles whose beliefs are founded upon a full knowledge of the ethos of his civilization, including its unwritten laws and modes of behavior, so that his actions have a frame of reference more ample and human than any rationale of conduct arbitrarily devised. Never fully embodied in any one character, this hero is implied throughout as the exemplary Southern gentleman of tradition. But Warren is not guilty in this of any nostalgic retreat into a romantic conception of the Old South; he is searching for modern meanings in its civilization, especially in its frontier strivings and its efforts to avert collapse today. As he says elsewhere (in an essay on Faulkner):

> The old order [in the South] . . . allowed the traditional man to define himself as human by setting up codes, concepts of virtue, obligations, and by accepting the risks of his humanity. Within the traditional order was a notion of truth, even if man in the flow of things did not succeed in realizing that truth.

With full recognition of all his imperfections, such a man could still be heroic. What counted was the human effort.

James F. Light

Structure, Meaning, and Technique in *All the King's Men*

Robert Penn Warren — poet, novelist, literary critic, magazine editor, and college professor — is a man of varied and impressive talents, but perhaps more than anything else he is a learned man. In his career as poet and novelist he wears his learning jauntily — witness the colloquial tone, at times verging onto the vulgar, of the narrator, Jack Burden, of *All the King's Men* — but Jack Burden's smart-alec pose does not lessen the fact that Warren is fundamentally a philosophic novelist. One of his philosophic novels is his masterpiece *All the King's Men* in which he tells two inter-related narratives. The first of these was undoubtedly inspired in part, though not in all its facts, by the personality and career of the demagogic Huey Long, the so-called Kingfish who dominated Louisiana politics before his assassination in the mid-1930's. In the novel the demagogue is named Willie Stark, and while Warren undoubtedly drew upon such other agitators as Mussolini for Willie's portrait, Willie's story is the archetypal one of the rise, corruption, and fall of the demagogue in any place and any time.

Willie's story begins in dreams and innocence. He is the hick from the country who believes in "law" and "justice," and who envisions aiding his fellow rednecks, the illiterate and semi-literate small farmers of Louisiana. As the populist "Abe Lincoln type,"[1] which is the phrase by which Jack Burden initially categorizes him, he enters politics in pursuit of his selfless ambition. He fights the good fight against corruption until by luck, and the collapse of a shoddily constructed school-building, he becomes a political hero. His desire to do good leads him to accept an invitation — he thinks of it as a "call" with all of the implications of that religious word — to run for Governor. In his innocence, both of himself and of human nature, he attempts to appeal to the illiterate populace by factual, logical speeches in which he asserts a program of social reform. No one listens to his speeches — no one seems to care for his dream of a better life for the rednecks to which he feels so bound — and he paces his room like a caged beast trying to find ways to make others listen. He is unsuccessful, however, until he learns that he is being used by corrupt politicians to split the farm-vote. When he learns this, he is born to a new identity. He takes his first drink of liquor, thus destroying the boy from the country who believed, with Jefferson, that people are inherently good, and beginning the end of the "country sap" who married the good, simple, religious school teacher named Lucy. A new being, "the Boss," is born, and Jack Burden makes the distinction between the "country sap" with ideals and the astute politician with power when he first meets the man for whom he eventually is to work. On the first meeting, Jack notes that someone named Alex had "the Boss" in tow: "Only it was not the Boss. Not to the crude eye of the *homme sensuel*. Metaphysically it was the Boss, but how was I to know?

---

[1] Robert Penn Warren, *All the King's Men* (New York, 1946), p. 23. Future page references to *All the King's Men* are to this edition and are given in parentheses in the text.

Fate comes walking through the door, and it is . . . wearing a seven-fifty seersucker suit . . . and a stiff high collar like a Sunday School superintendent. . . .It comes in just like that, and how are you to know (p. 16)?"

There are two beings then, and the second is born when the country sap takes his first drink and eventually passes out "cold," to use Warren's word, so that looking at him, Jack and Sadie Burke can refer to his "remains." The next morning Jack promises (in midwife terms) to "try to deliver" (p. 91) the body of Willie to the fair where Willie is to speak. That being which we learned earlier was inside Willie — "swelling and growing painfully and dully and imperceptibly like a great potato in a dark damp cellar" (p. 27) — is born into a new world, one of facts, relative morality, realism, expediency, and pragmatism.

The new being is a rednecked vulgarian who more and more begins to despise the common people, even while he wants to help them, and who appeals to the emotions, the desire for revenge of the populace. By rhetoric and promises the Boss gains his power and he clings to it, as Huey Long had done, by tactics of blackmail, bribery and terror. But "the Boss" is no simple, purely black villain. If he is a demagogue, he can claim, with some justification, that only a demagogue can be heard and be elected. If he is a destroyer — and his piercing political shout "Gimmee that meat-ax" (p. 147) proclaims that he is — he is, in part at least, a destroyer of a bad system: that of the exploitation of the state by gentlemen, with good manners and polite words, for the exclusive benefit of gentlemen. If he resorts to blackmail and to bribery, he at least can claim that such tactics are only realistic, men being what they are, and that the tactics are used for a good cause: the benefit medically, educationally, and socially of the many.

No, for Warren, Willie Stark is not a melodramatic villain. What he is is a stark, practical reality of the world. To use Jack Burden's phrase, Willie is "the man of fact" as opposed to his assassin, Adam Stanton, who is "the man of idea," and these two forces, asserts Burden, were "doomed to try to use the other and to yearn toward and try to become the other, because each was incomplete with the terrible division of the age" (p. 462). As the "man of fact," Willie has no delusions about the goodness of man; instead, he accepts the Puritan doctrine of the innate depravity of man — a doctrine which he asserts less theologically when he claims, "Man is conceived in sin and born in corruption and he passeth from the stink of the didie to the stench of the shroud" (p. 54). As a "man of fact," Willie can give a legal lesson to his Attorney General — one that sounds much like it came from such liberal jurists as Justices Holmes and Brandeis — when he claims that the law is never absolute but has to be continually revised to fit changing conditions. Willie colorfully expresses the relativistic theory of law, which states that law must fit the conditions of a particular time and place, when he tries to persuade Hugh Miller, his idealistic Attorney General, to accept the corruption of his administration: "The law is like the pants you bought last year for a growing boy, but it is always this year and the seams are popped and the shankbone's to the breeze. The law is always too short and too tight for growing humankind" (p. 145). Finally, as the "man of fact," Willie can preach to the "man of idea," Adam Stanton, the relativistic position on "goodness" and "badness." According to Willie, all things are made out of the bad, the dirt, because there is nothing else to make them out of. To such a statement Adam, from out of his moral absolutism, responds by asking, ' "How do you even recognize the good? Assuming you have made it from the bad? Answer me that." ' And Willie answers him, as a good relativist, by asserting, " 'You just make it up as you go along' " (p. 273). The answer so stuns Adam that he can't even understand it — ' "Make up what?" ' (p. 273) he asks — and Willie Stark elaborates on his answer in detail, concluding by claiming, ' "I'm not denying there's got to be a notion of right to get business done, but by God, any particular notion of any particular time will sooner or later get to be just like a stopper put tight in a bottle of water and thrown in a hot stove the way kids used to do at school to hear the bang" ' (p. 273). It is this practical, relativistic man that Jack Burden parrots when he tries to persuade Adam Stanton to do good—which is Adam's sole desire—by becoming the director of the hospital Willie plans to found. Adam's complaint that the hospital cannot be any good because its source, Willie, is bad parrots orthodox Puritan root-and-branch dogma and also echoes Christ's dictum, from the Sermon on the Mount, that "every good tree bringeth forth good fruit; but a corrupt tree bringeth forth evil fruit." Jack, however, destroys that argument, and in so doing leads Adam to begin to consider the job, by proclaiming the irrelevance of a source: "A thing is good in itself — if it is good. A guy gets ants in his pants and writes a sonnet. Is the sonnet less of a good . . . because the dame he got the ants over happened to be married to somebody else? . . ." ' (p. 252)

Willie Stark, then, is a practical politician, as well as a relativistic and pragmatic philosopher, but any man is not only what he is but what he was. What Willie Stark was once, before he became "the Boss," was a "country sap" who had been nurtured on Puritan theology and believed in some absolute idea of right and wrong. These older attributes cling to him like vestigial remnants even as he espouses his relativistic positions. Because such absolutist convictions are deeply inbred in him, he acts at times, even while he is "the Boss," in thorough opposition to his relativistic words. Jack Burden shows his awareness of this kind of illogic when he remembers Willie's desire to keep the Willie Stark hospital free of the corruption and profiteering of Tiny Duffy and Gummy Larson. Jack muses: "Now if Willie Stark believed that you always had to make the good out of the bad, why did he get so excited when Tiny just wanted to make a logical little deal with the hospital contract? Why did he get so heaped up just because Tiny's brand of Bad might get mixed in the raw materials from which he was going to make some Good. That was scarcely consistent" (p. 276). Obviously there is an inconsistency between Willie's rational, relativistic preachments and his occasional nonrational, intuitive actions. It is largely because of this non-rational man that the Boss, after his son's paralysis, decides to reform, to begin to leave the morass of dirt into which he's sunk. Deep within Willie, the non-rational man asserts the Old Testament concept of retribution for evil, and tells Willie that the paralysis of his son is the inevitable consequence of Willie's own actions; subconsciously Willie feels his own guilt in forcing the Louisiana football coach to play Tom Stark despite the fact that he has broken training and is out of condition. Out of Willie's guilt and his feeling of his own responsibility for the moral climate of the world, he abandons his mistresses, Sadie Burke and Anne Stanton, in order to return to his wife; and out of the same feeling, he breaks his word that he will allow the building contract for the Stark hospital to be granted to the corrupt contractor Larson. After Willie has told Larson's tool, Tiny Duffy, that Larson will not be given the contract, Jack Burden notes that Willie can walk all over Duffy but that Larson ' "is a different kind of cookie." ' To this Willie responds, " 'You got to start somewhere" ' (p. 411). Ironically, however, it is the reforming mood of Willie that brings about his assassination by the absolutist "man of idea" Adam Stanton, for Sadie Burke tells Tiny Duffy of Willie's affair with Anne Stanton, a fact which Duffy reports to Anne's brother Adam, who in his moral indignation and pristine purity assassinates Willie. Nonetheless, even on his death bed, Willie's sympathy for the "man of idea" asserts itself when he says, "He was all right. The Doc" ' (p. 424). And on his death bed, too, Willie dreams the dream so many men have had before him: that of a second chance. Dreaming that dream, he tells Jack, " 'It might have been all different . . . you got to believe that" ' (p. 425). But for Willie, as for all the others, there are only the consequences of what one has done in his one life; there is no second chance — save possibly in that others may learn from Willie's story, just as man, if he will, may learn from history.

That is one narrative strand of *All The King's Men*, but as Jack Burden asserts: "This has been the story of Willie Stark, but it is my story too. . . . It is the story of a man who lived in the world and to him the world looked one way for a long time and then it looked another and very different way" (p. 461).

The story of Jack is in part that of a traitor to his gentlemanly class. To show this, Warren insists on contrasting the aristocratic background of Jack Burden to the rednecked origins of Willie Stark. Despite his origins, Jack allies himself to the common people; yet, like Willie Stark, he cannot help despising their stupidity and their weakness, and he constantly sees the mass of the people as passive cows, dully ruminating while waiting to be milked.

Jack tells his story, as well as Willie's, from the vantage point in time of the middle-aged man who has married Anne Stanton, has seen and differentiated right and wrong, and is looking back and judging his youthful thoughts and actions as a journalist and as a henchman of Willie Stark's. The viewpoint — so similar to that of Fitzgerald's narrator in *The Great Gatsby* — is never obtrusive, but it does insist on its existence. Most especially, it does so through the chronological convolutions of time. This distortion of straight-forward chronology implies the inevitable causal linkage of events (in much the same way as does the manipulation of time in *The Great Gatsby*), and the viewpoint emphasizes the fallacy of many of the ideas of Jack Burden, the young smart-alec, as opposed to the ideas of Jack Burden, the mature man who has been educated by what he has seen of the realities of life. One brief example of this kind of contrast is Jack's thought in this early passage: "If the human race didn't remember anything it would be perfectly happy . . . if I learned anything from studying history that was what I learned. Or to be exact, that was what I thought I had learned" (p. 44). Obviously we are once again, as with Willie Stark, presented with the fact that there are two Jack Burdens, and once again we have numerous images of birth — though with Jack Burden the birth is strongly resisted. One such image occurs in the passage when Jack thinks of receiving a telegram:

> While you stand there in the hall, with the envelope in your hand, you feel there's an eye on you, a great big eye looking straight at you from miles and dark and through walls and houses and sees you huddled up way inside, in the dark which is you, inside yourself, like a clammy, sad little foetus you carry around inside yourself. The eye knows what's in the envelope, and it is watching you to see you when you open it and know, too. But the clammy, sad little foetus which is you down in the dark which is you too lifts up its sad little face and its eyes are blind, and it shivers cold inside you for it doesn't want to know what is in that envelope.(p. 11)

That passage implies Jack's ignorant foetal state — and his comfort in it — but the passage also suggests the end of that state when the foetus which is Jack, or you, "open[s] the envelope, for the end of man is to know" (p. 12). That is the journey Jack makes —from irresponsible ignorance to responsible knowledge—but it is a tortuous and painful journey, filled with personal tragedy, Freudian symbols of birth, and philosophic error. The tragedy and the rebirth come to a joint climax when the "bright, beautiful, silvery soprano scream" (p. 370) of Jack's mother, at the death of Judge Irwin, awakens Jack from sleep. Then he discovers that he has killed his own father (as, in Freudian terms, the son must metophorically kill the father to become his own man).

On his journey, before he comes to a final ethic, Jack also makes a number of philosophic errors. One of these is the philosophic idealism which he cynically asserts. For him, idealism posits the theory that everything exists in the mind, and all the things that seem to be going on out there in the external world are in actuality just shadow-reflections of the individual mind. If this is so, one can't be held morally accountable for harming or hurting others, for, as Jack asserts, "If you are an Idealist it doesn't matter what you do or what goes on around you because it isn't real anyway" (p. 33). Still a second of Jack's philosophic positions — before he learns better — is that man is but a machine, a collection of nerves, that inevitably responds as it must. To this theory — philosophically called mechanism — Jack gives the name The Great Twitch. Jack evolves his theory when, after he discovers Anne Stanton has become Willie Stark's mistress, he goes out West (implying the American dream that a new beginning can be found in the West), and he bases his theory on a man whose whole face seems to twitch independently of his mind. Jack then carries the theory to its ultimate conclusion. He does so by affirming that love is but a "mysterious itch" (p. 328) and that mind itself is really but a mechanical manifestation of the machine that is man and even of the machine that is the universe. Jack states his conclusion by asking and answering some questions: "Did the man's face know about the twitch and how it was all? And if I was all twitch how did the twitch which was me know that the twitch was all? Ah, I decided, that is the mystery. That is the secret knowledge. That is what you have to go to California to have a mystic vision to find out. That the twitch can know that the twitch is all. Then, having found that out, in the mystic vision, you feel clean and free. You are at one with the Great Twitch" (p. 334). With such a philosophy, Jack Burden can again disavow any personal responsibility, for "nobody had any responsibility for anything and there was no god but the Great Twitch" (p. 461). For Jack this naturalistic, mechanistic philosophy, so intimately associated with modern science and so dramatically fulfilled in the electrocautery surgery performed by Adam Stanton, "is the dream of our age" (p. 329). For Jack, there is, at first, horror in this mechanistic conception, much as there is in his discovery that a man's personality can be altered by electrocautery (note Jack's ironic contrast of this new, scientific method of conversion, only lacking baptism, with the older religious rituals). Later on, but before he gains real wisdom, there is for Jack a tonic effect in the new mechanistic philosophy, a reassurance of innocence in the rationalization that since you, or man, are but a machine "you are never guilty of a crime which you did not commit" (330).

Still a third of Jack's erroneous philosophical positions is that in which he rejects God by denying the concept of an infinite all-foreknowing Being. Mocking his apparent father, the weak Scholarly Attorney, who has contended that God is fullness of being — and therefore cannot move or change — Jack notes: "If God is Complete Knowledge then He is Complete Non-Motion which is Non-Life, which is Death. Therefore if there is such a God of Fullness of Being, we would worship Death, the Father" (p. 160). All of these philosophic positions, as Jack espouses them, serve as justifications, or rationalizations, of a completely amoral life — one that says by its way of living that a man can do anything, for nothing really matters anyway, and there is nothing resembling Truth, with a capital T, but only unrelated facts of existence. Believing in such a conception — though at times the despair inherent in it forces Jack into what he calls The Great Sleep — Jack can serve as Willie's researcher in ferreting out information for Willie to use for political blackmail. This activity Jack can even rationalize by claiming that he is a mere searcher for truth who can't be blamed because he doesn't make the evil he discovers. He can make such rationalizations, not because he's evil but because he's blind, and for him, as he says, the facts of the world, before he learned better, were but "a flux of things before his eyes . . . and one thing had nothing to do, in the end, with anything else" (p. 201). His attitude, for Warren, seems to be the consequence of a shallow irreligious mode of thought (one often identified with "science"), and it is out of such an attitude as Jack's that those men who made the atomic bomb could invent their creature and then disclaim any responsibility for its use. After all, they claimed, before guilt overcame them, they had nothing to do with the way the politicians used the bomb: they had only made it.

These are Jack's immature attitudes, expressions of his smart-alec cynicism, but from his ignorance he is born into knowledge. One step in his rebirth is the Ph.D. dissertation that he attempts to write on Cass Mastern. That story of his kinsman — whom he eventually, and ironically, learns is really unrelated to him — is a narrative of man's frailty, sinfulness, and hope of redemption. The tale exposes a truth, the moral responsibility that man holds for his actions, but Jack, though he is seeking it, is not yet mature enough to see that truth and finish the dissertation. What Cass Mastern learns, and what Jack Burden does not learn until the end of the novel, is expressed in one of the key images of the novel. Burden writes of his knowledge that the past changes the present, and that any action in the world has connection with other actions, when he notes from his vantage point in time:

> I have said that Jack Burden could not put down the facts about Cass Mastern's world because he did not know Cass Mastern. Jack Burden did not say definitely to himself why he did not know Cass Mastern. But I (who am what Jack Burden became) look back now, years later, and try to say why.
>
> Cass Mastern lived for a few years and in that time he learned that the world is all of one piece. He learned that the world is like an enormous spider web and if you touch it, however lightly, at any point, the vibration ripples to the remotest perimeter and the drowsy spider feels the tingle and is drowsy no more but springs out to fling the gossamer coils about you who have touched the web and then inject the black, numbing poison under your hide. It does not matter whether or not you meant to brush the web of things. Your happy foot or your gay ring may have brushed it ever so lightly, but what happens always happens and there is the spider, bearded black and with his great faceted eyes glittering like mirrors in the sun, or like God's eye, and the fangs dripping.
>
> But how could Jack Burden, being what he was, understand that? (p. 200)

In time Jack Burden learns what Cass Mastern had learned, but Jack learns it, as Cass had done and as each man must do, by the act of living, not in the scholar's study. For Jack, living becomes not an involvement with lust and slavery, as it had been for Cass Mastern, but an involvement with Willie Stark. This commitment suggests Jack's rejection of his genteel class, as well as his rejection of the Scholarly Attorney, his weakling father. Out of this involvement comes the supreme, and — in a Freudian sense — the liberating act of Jack's life. That event comes about through Jack's second important bit of historical research, a piece of inquiry which he entitles "The Case of the Upright Judge." In the course of this investigation, done at the instigation of Stark, Jack discovers that the man he most respects — the pure, venerable, aristocratic Judge Irwin — committed, out of his love for his home, a morally reprehensible act. When Jack confronts Judge Irwin with this fact, the Judge refuses to be blackmailed into supporting Willie Stark. Instead, he commits suicide, and the result of this act — in a novel which insists on the inextricable union of one act with another— is that Jack Burden discovers who his real father is. Beyond this, he learns that his father, Judge Irwin, was a mortal man and thus capable of sin, but also that he was a strong man worthy of respect, a man who "had not been good" — for he had cuckolded his friend and driven an unfortunate man to his death — but "had done good" (p. 374). In addition, Jack learns that his mother has the capacity for love, and out of that knowledge he gains a mother, for until now he has despised her as a cold and selfish being. With a loving mother and a strong father whom he can love, Jack can be truly reborn; the ice within him can begin "breaking up after a long winter. And the winter had been long"(p. 376). The midwife of his delivery is Truth, Knowledge, or Wisdom — call it what you will. Musing over this fact, Jack can think of how:

> by killing my father I had saved my mother's soul. Then I thought how maybe I had saved my father's soul, too. Both of them had found what they needed to know to be saved. Then I thought how all knowledge that is worth anything is paid for by blood. Maybe that is the only way you can tell that a certain piece of knowledge is worth anything: it has cost some blood (p. 455).

In probing into "The Case of the Upright Judge," Jack has uncovered knowledge but he has also discovered the inextricable linkage of past and present — the Judge's sin comes to haunt him years after the deed — as well as plumbed the mystery of man's moral responsibility for his actions. Because of this latter understanding Jack can realize that at times a lie is better than the truth, and can tell a lie which reassures his mother when she asks if there was an ignoble reason for the Judge's suicide. In telling that lie, Jack gives his mother a present, but he receives a gift in return from her: the strength to face the past. By lying, Jack shows that he has found the compassion which he previously lacked. That quality, that forgiveness for man's frailty, can make him realize that possibly those upright men who pretend to be unstained by sin are not as noble as they might wish, while those human beings — Willie Stark, Anne Stanton, Judge Irwin, even Tiny Duffy—who have been soiled by sin are still his brothers and worthy of love. The reason for this is that men are not perfect: if they were, they would be merely extensions of God, and God showed his greatness and his tolerance by creating something apart and different from himself. To say that man is less than God is not to deny, however, that man is morally responsible for what he does. He is, for Jack Burden has discovered that "History is blind [that is, morally neutral] but man is not" (p. 462). Man lives in the agony of will and the things he decides in 1971 may well have consequences in 1990 or even beyond. Man makes his life what it is, just as men make this world, and though, because of sin, man can never make this world paradise, he can make it better than it is. Jack Burden — who has learned the defects of pure moral absolutism and pure material relativism from Adam Stanton and Willie Stark — is, he says in the last lines of the novel, going out from his father's house "into the convulsion of the world, out of history into history and the awful responsibility of Time" (p. 464). He is going to be a committed man, holding the coat, he says, of Hugh Miller, who was once Attorney General for Willie Stark before Stark's dirty politics led to Miller's resignation.

Possibly Jack Burden, as the man who has learned both from the man of fact and the man of idea, may help in making a better world. To do so he must attempt to reconcile this real world of flux and motion with that other world of permanence and absolute perfection beyond; he must live in his Father's house, but be able to function in the world outside; he must be able to walk with his feet on the ground and his head in the skies. To do so he must become, in part at least, an old-time Puritan. That he is in the process of becoming so is implied by the responsibility which he assumes when he marries Anne Stanton and provides a home for his first "father," the scholarly attorney. In listening to the Puritanical tracts of the attorney, which are filled with the concepts of God's omnipotence and man's sinfulness, Jack Burden can even agree that "I was not certain, but that in my own way I did believe what he said" (p. 463).

To assert the Puritan in Warren does not alter, however, his supreme awareness that we live in a complex and impure world where simple black and white characters and events do not exist. For Warren the use of an evil means to achieve a good end may well destroy, morally, the agent seeking the good end, but the good will still remain. In expressing his conception of the "moral neutrality of history" Jack Burden speculates, undoubtedly with the characters and actions of the immoral pragmatist, Willie Stark, and the moral romanticist, Adam Stanton, in mind: "The morally bad agent may perform the deed which is good. The morally good agent may perform the deed which is bad. Maybe a man has to sell his soul to get the power to do good" (p. 418). In such a mixed up world, there is constant irony and paradox. Judge Irwin, out of an excess of love for his home at the Landing, commits the sin which destroys him. Governor Stanton, out of an excess of friendship for Judge Irwin, stains his own honor (" 'his failing' " claims Judge Irwin, " 'was a defect of his virtue' " [p. 369]). Willie in a desire to reform — " 'You got to start somewhere,'" ' he tells Jack—decides to keep the Willie Stark Hospital completely pure, breaks his promise to Gummy Larson to allow some graft in the construction of the hospital, and thus sets off the chain of actions that leads to his own murder.

In this muddled world, where, as Jack Burden says, "The good comes out of the bad and the bad out of the good, and the devil take the hindmost" (p. 263), it often seems that it is better to sin, in conventional terms, than to live in purity and innocence. That point is made in larger terms in the contrast between Willie Stark and Adam Stanton (for certainly, from Warren's point of view, Willie Stark brings more "good" into being than does Adam Stanton) but is is also made in smaller ones in the drama of Jack Burden's love affair with Anne Stanton. Having grown up with Anne, Jack retains and is later paralyzed by a childhood image of her which symbolizes to him her perfect innocence. An obsessively recurrent image for him is one of her floating on water, under a dark purple sky, with a white gull crossing very high. Because of this image, Jack is morally unable to seduce her when he has the opportunity. To do so wouldn't be "right" he tells her, and later on he remembers "the surprise I felt when I heard that word there in the air . . . I couldn't any more have touched her than if she had been my little sister" (p. 313). Often afterwards, Jack comforts himself with his nobility towards Anne, but after she has become Willie Stark's mistress and has thus destroyed Jack's image of her innocence, Jack thinks that if he had acted differently and had completed his seduction of her, they would, by their joint "sin," have discovered in Puritan, Haw- thornean terms, their brotherhood in the common guilt of man.[2]

By implication, therefore, Anne, if she had been seduced, would have married Jack and never have become Willie's mistress, and Jack would never have gone West to discover the Theory of The Great Twitch. Thinking of that irony of the uncompleted seduction,

---

[2] In an article to which I am much indebted, "The Narrator's Mind as Sym- bol: An Analysis of *All The King's Men*," *Accent*, VII (Summer 1947), Norton R. Girault also makes the point of Jack Burden's reluctance to be born into a world of common guilt: "His hesitation in his love affair with Anne Stanton results, in part, from the same sort of recoil from knowledge. And his dive and underwater embrace with her are an attempt to submerge himself also with Anne in a cozy womb-state of 'not knowing.' (The medium will not retain them, of course, and they burst forth into their separateness.) Finally, this subconscious shrinking from a particular kind of knowledge becomes on Jack's part an attempt to repudiate his sensibility, an attempt begun as a result of his frustration in his love affair with Anne and of his dissatisfaction with his past (as symbolized by his parents). On the verge of the sexual act with Anne, he had sensed that to 'know' Anne he would have to violate his image of her; he hesitates long enough to disrupt their love affair.

"What Jack is searching for is a womb-state of innocence in nature in which his image of Anne will be preserved. And this search becomes a dominant motif leading up to his expulsion from the womb when he unwittingly causes the death of his father. Just before his discovery that Anne has become the Boss's mistress, he sits in his office and envies the jaybird perched in the tree outside his window: 'I could look down and think of myself inside that hollow cham- ber, in the acqueous green light, inside the great globe of the tree, and not even a jaybird there with me now, for he had gone, and no chance of seeing anything beyond the green leaves, they were so thick, and no sound except, way off the faint mumble of traffic, like the ocean chewing its gums.' The associations with Jack's underwater dive with Anne are significant. Then, when this reverie is interrupted by his discovery of Anne's 'infidelity' (of the Boss's violation of the image), Jack flies to California in an attempt to 'drown himself in West.' In all these struggles to lose himself in nature, there is a paradoxical struggle toward rebirth: the greater the struggle to resist rebirth, the greater the counter- struggle toward rebirth, as if Jack's nature, unformed, were enveloped by the womb of total nature, which reacts convulsively to reject him. Through his attempts to lose himself in nature, Jack is actually struggling, without realizing it, toward a discovery of his separateness in nature.

"The significance of Jack's struggle to resist rebirth may be stated in these terms: Jack shrinks from the discovery of evil, of the taint in nature, of im- perfection in the scheme of things. He has seen ugliness and imperfection and, with a cynical smugness, acknowledges their presence in nature but he does not want to discover evil in himself. Subconsciously, he shrinks from the terrible knowledge that he is capable of good and evil, but until he is reborn through a revelation of the guilt he shares with humanity, he is not fully man, but rather embryonic and amoral."

Jack sees that "any nobility (or whatever it was) had had in my world as dire a consequence as Cass Mastern's sin had had in his" (p. 315). Even more ironically, this thought of what might have been occurs before the further consequence of Anne's liaison with Willie: before Adam Stanton, whose desire for perfect innocence has also been traumatically destroyed by his sister's act, murders Willie Stark out of the conviction that he epitomizes the total corruptness of this world. All hangs together; and carried far enough, Jack Burden's uncommitted seduction, his unfulfilled lust, can be viewed as having caused as tragic a consequence, in the murder of Willie and the death of Adam, as that sin of fulfilled lust committed when Cass Mastern betrayed his friend Duncan Trice and coupled with Trice's wife almost a hundred years before.

In a novel of sin, betrayal, and guilt, where the first image is one of motion, where the last word is Time, where the entirety of the action of the novel is implicit in the first chapter and where the central thesis is the complex interweaving of past, present, and future, there seems to be a Whitmanesque lesson. That preachment says something about the obligation each man has to his fellows, even to that great passive cow, the slowly, dully, ruminating people. But the lesson extends beyond that obligation to the responsibility that each man, each civilization has to the future. Out of the past and into the present, we forever go forward into the future. That future is determined by all that precedes it — such is "the awful responsibilty of time" — and if there is any hope for a better future, it is based on the possibility that man may learn from history, may accept his brotherhood in guilt (as Jack does when he imagines that Tiny Duffy winks at him in brotherly comradeship), and may then recognize the need in this world for compassion, love, and social commitment. Through the recognition of these things, as well as through the willingness to live by them, each man may make his life worth the living, and, in so doing, may also aid the possibility of human survival. It was the lack of these things in Jack Burden that made Anne Stanton unwilling to marry him; it is his growth in humanity that ultimately makes the success of that marriage possible.

Because Jack Burden has learned the lesson of compassion, love, and social commitment, the novel ends not in despair but in restrained optimism. That note is also emphasized by the epigraph of the novel: "Mentre che la speranzo ha fior del verde." From Dante's *Purgatorio* III, 135 (Per lor maladizion si non si perde/che non possa torna l'etterno amore,/*Mettre che las speranza ha fior del verne./* No man may be so cursed/that Eternal Love cannot still return/while any thread of green still lives in hope), the epigraph is spoken by Dante's character Manfred. Doomed to purgatory for his iniquitous sins, he is successfully undergoing purgation, and he preaches the grace of God while he dreams of redemption and salvation through God's mercy and love. In a similar way, Jack Burden acts as if he believes that through compassion (given to his mother and the "scholarly attorney"), through love (for his father and his wife), and through his sense of social commitment (to be fulfilled with Hugh Miller), he may redeem his past sins, find peace, and build a life in this world that may justify the hope of one beyond.[3] That kind of hope, sentimental and old fashioned as it may be, comes not from the new religion of science but from the old faith of our fathers preached by the scholarly attorney when he claims: "The creation of evil is therefore the index of God's glory and His power. That had to be so that the creation of good might be the index of man's glory and power. But by God's help. By His help and in His Wisdom" (p. 463). Warren, like Jack Burden at the end of the novel, believes, in his own way, in such a faith.

---

[3] For a fuller discussion of the relevance of the epigraph to the comparison between Manfred and Jack Burden, see Earl Wilcox, *"Warren's All The King's Men*, epigraph," *The Explicator* (December, 1967), item 29.

Malcolm O. Sillars

A Study in Populism

All the King's Men, Robert Penn Warren's novel of the Southern demagogue and the men and women around him, has been examined from many points of view. It may be worthwhile to examine some of the too often overlooked socio-economic implications of the novel. All the king's men, and the king himself, can be clearly seen to represent the great American tradition of Populism that swept the poorer agricultural areas of the Middle West and the South in the late 1930's. It is surely far more than the narrow context of the life of

---

Reprinted from *American Quarterly*, IX (Fall, 1957), 345-53, by permission of the journal and the author. Copyright © 1957 by the Trustees of the University of Pennsylvania.

Huey Long, as too many have mistakenly supposed. The spirit of
Willie Stark has reared itself in many states and in many forms; in
Bloody Bridles Waite of Colorado, Sockless Jerry Simpson of
Kansas, William Jennings Bryan of Nebraska, Alfalfa Bill Murray
of Oklahoma, Kissin' Jim Folsom of Alabama and many others. The
political elements of *All the King's Men* are rooted in the past and
yet are all, in one way or another, degenerative of the tradition
they represent.

There are four such elements which should be isolated and their
interrelationships known in order to see more clearly the novel's
meaning. The hill people of the South represent a particular economic group who are now, as they were in the days of Willie Stark,
and earlier in the days of Pitchfork Ben Tillman, set apart from the
more aristocratic and proper conservative people of the flatlands.
Willie Stark is an example of the leaders produced by the hills to do
battle on their behalf. The political position of the aristocrats of the
Delta illuminates Stark's rise and fall. Jack Burden is an aristocrat
who loses, then finds himself in trying to bridge the gap between the
hills and the Delta.

I

Essential to the understanding of Willie Stark is an understanding
of the social construct which produced him. The hill people are a
crucial phenomenon in the economic and social structure of middle-
western and southern agricultural areas. The geographical dividing
line between hills and black belt only serves to draw into sharper
focus, in the South more than elsewhere, the economic battle. These
hill people are holders of small plots of poor red farmland from which
they eke out an existence of amazing stubbornness and an evangelical Protestant code of ethics. They see themselves as the chosen
people who do battle with the more prosperous, and evil Delta
planters. They are fiercely individualistic.

They were less inclined to favor the Civil War because they had
less interest in Negro slavery. They were more susceptible to Populism with its interest in freeing the small farmer from the control of
the bankers, railroads, elevator operators and other more well-to-do
elements of the society. They were more likely to break from Al
Smith on the issues of Catholicism and Prohibition because the
economic issue was less pronounced in 1928 and so provided them
with a chance to vote religion and liquor. They supported the New
Deal and in the election of 1948 they endorsed the Democratic party

more than did the Delta, which found the politics of the New and
Fair Deals threatening their power position by raising the standards
of the Negroes and the rednecks of the hills. [1]

The same Populist sentiment was strong in the Corn Belt and for
similar reasons. In the South it was rocky red soil; in Kansas and
Nebraska it was rainfall. In the late nineteenth century there was
real correlation between the amount of rainfall and the intensity of
Populist fervor in western Nebraska. [2] *All the King's Men* is the
product of a socio-economic vortex which reduced a proud people to
desperate action.

The hill people have a concept of good and evil by which they see
themselves as the chosen people who have had their birthright
stolen. To the Populist, as to most liberals, good and evil are concen-
trated. One attribute is found in one group and one in another. Or,
the individual is good and governments, or corporations or bankers
or what have you, are evil. Thus, reasons the liberal, return the
society to its natural owners and there will be peace in the land. The
hill people, with Presbyterian rigidity, see the inhabitants of the
Delta living a riotous life of drunken orgies, during which time they
spend on booze and vain, heartless women, the money that the tax
collector, the banker, the railroad agent and the grain elevator steals
from the children of the hills. Their strong religious backgrounds
also cause them to be more susceptible to the Messiah. And this
Messiah, they believe, will always rise from among them (a false
conclusion if we examine the backgrounds of the men who have
actually acted positively for these people — Jefferson, Jackson and
F. D. Roosevelt).

One of the lessons to be learned from *All the King's Men* is that
these conditions still exist and this latent evangelical liberalism is
always present. In 1948 Henry Wallace (a curious combination of
populist and aristocrat) tried to exploit this agrarian liberalism with
his "Gideon's Army" and his promises to the "little people." His
liberalism had lost its roots, however, and the stronger urban liberalism which dominated the Wallace campaign was not acceptable to
rural people. Further, in 1948 Wallace had in Harry S. Truman, an
opponent who better fit the picture of the hill people's leader. The
conditions — economic, social and religious — which formed the

[1] Perhaps the best explanation of this condition is found in V. O. Key, "Alabama: Planters, Populists, 'Big Mules,'" *Southern Politics* (New York: Alfred
A. Knopf, 1949), chap. iii.
[2] John D. Hicks, *The Populist Revolt* (Minneapolis: The University of Min-
nesota Press, 1931), pp. 30-35.

amalgam producing Willie Stark are a significant part of American history. They should be studied in a dispassionate light for insights into the future.

II

Willie Stark, the leader produced by the conditions and prejudices of the hill people, is second of the important social elements in Robert Penn Warren's novel, for while Willie Stark is an individual, he is also an institution. He has all the background and beliefs of the hill people mentioned earlier. As county treasurer he sacrifices his political life in a fight to see that the courthouse gang in Mason City does not make the new schoolhouse a political plum. His opponents tell the people that the company submitting the lowest bid would bring in Negroes from the lowlands and thus deprive the local people of jobs. Incidentally, they tell the people that the Negroes would be the common laborers. Essentially this is the point at which the hill people always break with the Negroes. They do not have as many to contend with as in the flat country and so do not fear their political power as the aristocrats do. But when the Negro threatens them economically, race becomes an issue. Willie fights but loses. Other real life Willie Starks are destroyed politically in just such a manner.

The fire escape of the schoolhouse, built of inferior materials, falls during a fire drill and three children are killed. Willie is thus made a political power. He had warned them about what the courthouse gang was trying to do and he was right. With this he advances to the second step in the rise of the redneck leader, what Professor V. O. Key calls the "friends and neighbors" politician. [3] In the hills around Mason City he is a political power. His is the protest for the inarticulate people of the area.

His rise to statewide prominence comes when Willie again sacrifices himself politically. Convinced of his popularity he is induced to enter the race for Governor by Tiny Duffy, the perfect stereotype of the smalltown political boss. During the campaign, Stark discovers that he has been nominated to take votes from MacMurfee, a candidate who is also popular in the hills. Willie goes to the political rally, rather symbolically pushes Tiny Duffy off the platform and reveals his part in the act. He tells the people to vote for MacMurfee and not for him. He tells them to sit in judgment on MacMurfee and remove

---

[3] Key, *Southern Politics,* p. 37.

him if he is wrong. MacMurfee wins the election. Willie, by this sacrifice, becomes a state-wide figure. He fits the standards of honesty that the hill people want and becomes their champion. He was duped as they had been, time and time again.

Probably of interest here is the change in the spoken rhetoric of Willie Stark. Previous to this time Stark talked about issues, about specific problems of taxes, education and roads. His speeches were clearly dull and unemotional. When he speaks at the rally he speaks to the emotional needs of the hill people. One might reflect that this was Willie's awakening, or rebirth if you will, to the realities of political power and the first step to his destruction. I do not, however, place such an interpretation on the act. Willie is here telling the truth and in the language the Hills understand.

MacMurfee, of course, fails to live up to the promises of the election and the inevitable wave of the future sweeps Willie into the Governor's Mansion. But Willie is different from the rest. He cannot be bought by political machines. Instead he forms his own machine and like too few others who rose in a similar manner, he actually goes about attempting to solve the problems of the hill people. He builds highways, schools and hospitals. He raises the taxes of the rich (the lowland aristocrats) and defends the hill people in the courts.

The greatest fight is the one which Willie goes through in relating his past to realities of politics. He finds out that there is both good and evil in all men. Byram B. White, as State Auditor, dips his hand into the till and Willie is shaken up. The little man from the hills is just as capable of evil as the folks of the lowlands. Not that putting one's hand into the till is so bad — for Willie had come now to realize that this is an essential part of the machinery of political power, but White does it behind Willie's back. In short, he is disloyal to the cause which Willie represents. And White's willingness to write an undated resignation deepens Stark's realization of his power over men.

> "I gave him every chance," the boss said glumly. "Every chance. He didn't have to say what I told him to say. He didn't have to listen to me. He could have just walked out the door and kept on walking. He could have done a dozen things. But did he? Hell, no. Not Byram, and he just stands there and his eyes blink right quick like a dog's do when he leans up against your leg before you hit him, and, by God, you have the feeling if you don't do it, you won't be doing God's will. You do it because you are helping Byram fulfill his nature."

Out of his experiences there grows the conclusion that life is not just a clash of good and evil but rather (returning selectively to his fundamentalist Sunday school) all evil. As Willie Stark puts it, "Man is conceived in sin and born in corruption and he passeth from the stink of the didie to the stench of the shroud."

This conviction influences Willie's concept of progress profoundly. His real concern is with the problem of producing that which is good. He reveals this in his exchange with the intellectual and idealistic Dr. Adam Stanton.

> "There is one question I should like to ask you." [Said Stanton.] "It is this. If, as you say, there is only the bad to start with, and the good must be made from the bad, then how do you ever know what the good is? How do you even recognize the good? Assuming you have made it from the bad. Answer me that."
> "Easy, Doc, easy," the Boss said.
> "Well, answer it."
> "You just make it up as you go along."
> "Make up what?"
> "The good," the Boss said. "What the hell else are we talking about. Good with a capital G."

His political philosophy thus completed, Willie runs roughshod over everyone who gets in his way.

Indicative of his change in philosophy, there is a degeneration in Willie Stark's oral rhetoric. The genuine Populist cry for justice is dissipated into demagoguery. Observe Theodore Bilbo in actual life as cited by V. O. Key in *Southern Politics*.

> In 1934, Bilbo brought into play his genius for rough-and-tumble campaigning. He wore, from an earlier campaign, a scar won in his oratorical battles for the people. He had been rapped over the head with a pistol butt by an opponent whom he had described as a "cross between a hyena and a mongrel . . . begotten in a nigger graveyard at midnight, suckled by a sow, and educated by a fool." In the 1934 campaign as in others, Bilbo — who had earlier done a little Baptist preaching — salted his oratory with bastard King Jamesian orotundities, long familiar to his audiences from the sermons of their evangelical preachers: "Friends, fellow citizens, brothers and sisters — hallellujah. — My opponent — yea, this opponent of mine who has the dastardly, dewlapped, brazen, sneering, insulting and sinful affrontery to ask you for your votes without telling you the people of Mississippi what he is a-going to do with them if he gets them — this opponent of mine says he don't need a platform . . . He

asks, my dear brethren and sisters, that you vote for him because he is standing by the President. . . . I shall be the servant and Senator of all the people. . . . The appeal and petition of the humblest citizen, yea, whether he comes from the black prairie lands of the east or the alluvial lands of the fertile delta; yea, he will be heard and my feet shall be swift, . . . your Senator whose thoughts will not wander from the humble, God-fearing cabins of Vinegar Bend, . . . your champion who will not lay his head upon his pillow at night before he has asked his Maker for more strength to do more for you on the morrow . . . Brethren and sisters, I pledge . . ."[4]

There is further degeneration in Willie. It is exemplified by his infidelity to his wife, Lucy. Lucy, the prime mover in Willie's earlier high moral purpose, is relegated to the position of a publicity piece. She is used for the furtherance of the Governor's political ends. For sexual satisfaction Willie turns to a collection of women who are not the product of the hills. In short, Willie falls into the very pattern of life in his personal affairs which the hill people have hated (or perhaps envied) in the people of the lowlands—heavy drinking and infidelity. In the end it is Anne Stanton's brother Adam who kills Willie when he finds out that his sister had been Willie's mistress. Thus, Willie's failure to do the impossible and fulfill the picture which the redneck has of his leaders caused his downfall.

Despite Stark's actions, the wool hat boys never desert him. Even more significant, the clear-thinking Lucy doesn't either. When their wild-living son Tom is paralyzed in a football accident — a symbol of Willie's attempt and failure to construct a pleasant world — Lucy is there to help Willie on with his coat and take him home. After the deaths of Willie and Tom, Lucy adopts a child born to the promiscuous Sibyl Frey with a conviction born of faith that it is Tom Stark's illegitimate son. The name for the boy: Willie — Willie Stark. With all that she has been put to personally in Governor Stark's rise and fall, she knows as the hill people know that there is something in Willie which must be preserved. Thus, as the novel ends, Lucy Stark represents the inarticulate hill people who must have faith in their Willie Stark because experience has taught them that there is no other source for their salvation. And Willie knows also, perhaps for the first time clearly, on his death bed as he says — "It could have been different."

Thus, in death, Willie Stark returns to his roots. There is a solution to the evils of the society in which the hill people live and the

---

[4] Key, *Southern Politics*, pp. 242-43.

solution is in the conquest of political power by an articulate spokes-
man who will act. Whether or not this belief is correct is not an issue.
The real point is that the hopes and aspirations of these people are
genuine and Willie's attempts to meet these needs are also genuine.
It is in the red dirt and man's weaknesses that Willie's failures are
rooted. The fallacy of Populism, and perhaps of all liberalism then,
is the fallacy of not understanding nature.

III

The third social element in the novel is the aristocracy of the
Delta. Like the geographical division between the hills and the
plains, the aristocracy of the deep South is more clearly defined than
in other sections of the country. On the plains of the deep South, the
plantation owners have built a tradition of aristocratic conservatism.
They use political power to protect a social system which is grounded
in stability and respect for law. It is from this area that most of the
great leaders of the South have come to contribute to American
government in the fields of finance and foreign policy. But with all of
their respectability they have almost always been lax in their willingness to help the poor farmers of the hills. They are the evil which the
hill people see and react to. Because of the code and tradition of
these people they do not understand Willie Stark. In *All the King's
Men* Judge Irwin of Burden's Landing is the personification of this
school of thought. Judge Irwin is the best of his tradition. He, unlike
many of the more complacent men and women of the area, sees a
need for social improvement. However, the judge is in a dilemma.
The society which he represents will not allow change without the
overt pressure of Willie Stark. Thus, there is no conservative way to
solve problems, it seems. There is only Willie Stark's way and this
is unacceptable to the judge.

Robert Penn Warren goes beyond this weakness, however, to show
that even the people of the plain, when the hard crust of conservative
respectability is removed, are not without corruption. Judge Irwin,
while he was Attorney General, was involved in a kickback scheme
which eventuated in the suicide of Mortimer L. Littlepaugh, Counsel
for the American Electric Power Company. Governor Stanton had
known of the action and shielded Irwin. The rectitude which is so
lauded in the aristocracy is really only a facade. They are not above
corruption when they find it necessary. This element dramatizes the
sin of the aristocracy. Their real sin is their failure to recognize and
alleviate the economic conditions of the poorer people of the hills.

Thus, in the South as well as elsewhere, the aristocracy has a respectable legal conservatism. They contribute greatly by giving powerful and intelligent leadership to the nation. But their conservatism is seldom respectable in dealing with the real socio-economic problems of the area and their legality is constructed to control such socio-economic improvement.

IV

The fourth element in the novel is Jack Burden. From the standpoint of the political nature of the agrarian areas he is significant as a touchstone moving between the hills and the black belt. Jack Burden is a product of the aristocracy. His early association with Judge Irwin makes a great impression on him. His youth is spent with Anne and Adam Stanton. All the elements of his life are linked to the Delta, but his realization that there is something unsatisfactory in this self-satisfied existence sets him adrift. Given the chance to work for Willie Stark, he accepts and quickly falls in with all the activities which characterize Willie. His actions in working to find ammunition for Willie's plans eventually bring him to attack the very roots from which he sprang. Through his revelation of Judge Irwin's and Governor Stanton's actions he destroys the very people who had previously meant the most to him, Adam Stanton, Anne Stanton and Judge Irwin. Anne Stanton becomes Willie Stark's mistress, Adam Stanton kills Willie and is killed himself by Willie's bodyguard and Judge Irwin commits suicide.

Burden seems lost in his conviction that there is no code of ethics or morals but only the "big twitch." Although Willie feels that Jack is the only person who really knows him, Jack realizes that he does not understand Willie at all. Perhaps the products of the aristocracy can never really understand the hill people and their kind of leadership.

As the novel draws to a climax, Jack Burden looks through the cloud of action without purpose in which he has been existing and begins to see clearly. He does, in the end, bridge the gap. There can be, he seems to know, a connection between the hills and the Delta. There can be respect for law and at the same time socio-economic progress. As the novel ends he is telling the reader that he may get back into politics. If so, it will be to help Hugh Miller who resigned as Attorney General when Governor Stark refused to fire Byram B. White. Miller is the symbol of the very leadership which is necessary, a man of respectability who wishes to use the law to help the people.

V

In surveying the rise and fall of a Populist politician and the people who support and oppose him, *All the King's Men* leaves the reader with the hope of Lucy Stark. Another Willie will come along and he will not fall into the snare of demagoguery, blackmail and thuggery. Contemporary politics would seem to show us that this is possible. George Norris in Nebraska and Bob La Follette in Wisconsin are clear examples of this tradition. And in the South, examples of respectable Populism like John Sparkman and Lister Hill of Alabama prove that agrarian democrats can be law abiding. Further, the enlightened conservatism of such men as Fulbright of Arkansas adds awareness to respectability. It is also true that shortsighted conservatism still exists in the agrarian areas in the personages of Thurmond, Byrnes, Byrd and the like. It is further true that Populism has gone sour of late not only in Huey Long and Theodore Bilbo but most recently in Joseph McCarthy of Wisconsin. But the gap can be bridged either by a Populist who climbs up or an aristocrat who bends down. This is the essential lesson of *All the King's Men* and perhaps of America.

Robert White

Robert Penn Warren and the Myth of the Garden

Although it is in his recent long narrative poem, *A Brother to Dragons*, that Robert Penn Warren has most explicitly examined some of the attitudes and cherished beliefs of Americans toward their own past, such a concern has been prominent in much of his earlier poetry and in the greater part of his fiction. In large measure, much of his poetry and fiction has been directed toward an examination of what Henry Nash Smith has termed the "myth of the

Reprinted from *Faulkner Studies*, III (Winter, 1954), 59-67, by permission of *Critique Magazine*.

garden." Of course, many American writers have been concerned with the past, have found notable ideals in the past, and have compared that past with their present. But Warren has been quite unlike most other writers in his treatment of the American experience.

Generally speaking, one might say that the story of modern American literature is a double story. A story of an attempt to idealize the past, the past in which society was predominantly rural and agrarian and supposedly more moral and virtuous and democratic; and the story of a disillusioned and despairing outcry against modern industrial society, which supposedly has done away with the American dream and promise, which has blasted the innocence and hope that were ours before the advent of the twentieth century. Such idealization and disillusionment may be found not only in such mediocre writers as Thornton Wilder and Stephen Benet, but in such writers as Sherwood Anderson, William Faulkner, and F. Scott Fitzgerald. The anguished cry of betrayal is perhaps most poignantly expressed in the final passage of *The Great Gatsby*, when Nick Carraway stands in the moonlight and becomes aware "of the old island here that flowered once for Dutch sailors' eyes — a fresh, green breast of the new world. Its vanished trees, the trees that made way for Gatsby's house, had once pandered in whispers to the last and greatest of all human dreams."

Warren sees the green breast of the new world differently. He speaks of the "heyday of hope and heart's extravagance," when the settlers poured over the Appalachians into the fertile river valleys of Kentucky, as a time

> When Grab was watchword and earth spread her legs
> Wide as she could, like any jolly trollop
> Or bouncing girl back in the brushes after
> The preaching or the hustling bee, and said,
> "Come git it, boy, hit's yourn, but get it deep.

Americans have rarely chosen to think of the rich and fertile earth as a jolly trollop. They have rather chosen to personify the land in the flowing garb and stately manner of a Ceres. Or they have thought of the land, the virgin land of the forest, as an unfulfilled vision or as Frederick Jackson Turner's life-giving cradle of democracy. Such images of the land are deep at the core of what may be called the American faith, the American mythology.

Much of Warren's poetry and fiction is concerned with two of the most persistent and dominant elements in this mythology — the belief in the moral efficacy of a now almost entirely vanished agrarian

mode of life, in the moral virtues of the frontiersman and the hus-
bandman; and the hallowed belief in the possibilities of a rational
and benevolent democracy. This concern may be seen in the early
"Ballad of Billie Potts," where the tragedy is acted out against the
backdrop of the push to the West, but where there is no idealization
of the pioneers, "the slush and swill of the world's great pot/That
foamed at the range's lip, and spilled/Like quicksilver across green
baize." The concern may also be seen in the two early novels, *Night
Rider* and *At Heaven's Gate*, particularly in the former novel, in the
treatment of the trapper, Willie Proudfit, who goes West and lives
among the Indians, but who finds that there is no innocence in prim-
itivism. But I am here going to deal only with the two later novels,
All the King's Men and *World Enough and Time*.

It would be foolish to assert that *All the King's Men* deals primarily with either the myth of the garden or the westward push of the
pioneers. But the novel (which is, I think, primarily concerned with
a split in the consciousness of modern man equivalent to the split
between the back-to-back attitudes of idealism and cynicism) does
deal with these themes; and Warren's treatment of them is consist-
ently unsentimental and undisillusioned. The locale of the novel
is hardly a garden, of either a physical or a socio-moral variety. The
landscape may be described in clean, incisive, unhortatory terms.

> A hundred yards off, at the foot of the rise, there was a patch of
> woods, scrub oak and such. The ground must have been swampy
> down there, for the grass and bare ground beyond it looked too
> green to be natural . . . I leaned on the fence and looked off west
> across the country where the light was stretching out, and breathed
> in that dry, clean, ammoniac smell you get around stables at sun-
> set on a summer day.

Or it may be described (all the description, of course, comes through
the first person narrative of Jack Burden) in terms that are somewhat more floreate but which do not at all imply that nature is a
good and benevolent force.

> A month from now, in early April, at the time when far away, outside
> the city, the water hyacinths would be covering every inch of bayou,
> lagoon, creek, and backwater, with a spiritual-mauve to obscene-
> purple, violent, vulgar, fleshy, solid, throttling mass of bloom over
> the black water, and the first heart-breaking misty green like child-
> hood dreams, on the old cypresses would have settled down to be
> leaf and not a damned thing else . . . and the insects would come

boiling out of the swamp and day and night the whole air would vibrate with them with a sound like an electric fan.

Warren's attitudes toward both nature and the oftentimes supposed conflict between industrialism and agrarianism can be well seen in his treatment of the object-symbols of industrialism seen against the backdrop of nature. The paean to the internal combustion engine,

> . . . . this is the country where the age of the internal combustion engine has come into its own. Where every boy is Barney Oldfield, and the girls . . . have smooth little faces to break your heart and when the wind of the car's speed lifts up their hair at the temples you see the sweet little beads of perspiration nestling there . . . Where the smell of gasoline and burning brake bands and red-eye is sweeter than myrrh,

may be taken as an ironic commentary on its essential destructiveness, but such an interpretation is only likely when the reader is already committed to a set of preconceived notions about the evils of gasoline. Taken plainly, the passage is a celebration of the automobile; Warren does not suggest, as Faulkner has done, that the "Barney Oldfields" would be better off following a mule down a furrow. The girls nestling close to the dashboard have "smooth little faces" and the perspiration at their temples is "sweet."

However, generally, the automobile and other symbols of an industrial society are not so much celebrated as they are recorded, with an almost indifferent dispassionateness. This may be seen in the following description of Willie Stark's Cadillac hurtling through the night.

> We would go gusting along the slab . . . Close to the road a cow would stand knee-deep in the mist, with horns damp enough to have a pearly shine in the starlight, and would look at the black blur we were as we went whirling into the blazing corridor of light . . . .The cow would stand there knee-deep in the mist and look at the black blur and the blaze and then, not turning its head, at the place where the black blur and the blaze had been, with the remote, passive, unvindictive indifference of God-All-Mighty or Fate or me, if I were standing there knee-deep in the mist.

Nature is indifferent to the machine, for there is really no conflict between the two. Such a conflict can only possess an imagined existence in the mind of man, a conflict built up by man in an attempt to escape from the actualities of involvement in a world of men. The futility of thinking in such terms is expressively stated in the passage where Jack Burden looks from the window of the train carrying him away from the town where Willie Stark has finally discovered that he has been played for a sucker. He watches a woman fling a pan of water from a back door and as the speed of the train picks up,

> . . . . its effort seems to be through a stubborn cloying density of air as though an eel tried to swim in syrup, or the effort seems to be against an increasing and implacable magnetism of earth. You think that if the earth would twitch once, as the hide of a sleeping dog twitches, the train would be jerked over and piled up and the engine would spew and gasp . . . . But nothing happens, and you remember that the woman had not even looked up at the train. You forget her, and the train goes fast, and it is going fast when it crosses a little trestle. You catch the sober metallic, pure, late-light, unriffled glint of the water between the little banks, under the sky, and see the cow standing in the water upstream under the single leaning willow.

There is no conflict between woman and the machine, or between nature and the machine. The woman doesn't even look at the train and the cow stands indifferently under the trestle.

In this novel, Warren quite interestingly examines some of the implications of America's push westward. After Jack Burden discovers that Anne Stanton is Willie Stark's mistress, when his ideal of Anne is shattered, he flees West, drowns himself in the West.

> For West is where we all plan to go someday. It is where you go when the land gives out; the old-field pines encroach. It is where you go when you get the letter saying: *Flee, all is discovered.* It is where you go when you look down at the blade in your hand and see the blood on it. It is where you go when you are told that you are a bubble on the tide of empire.

Jack goes to the continent's end, to Long Beach, California, "the essence of California," so that his body might "sink down to the very bottom of West and lie in the motionless ooze of History." As he lies there, drinking and watching the flicker of a neon sign, he relives the tragic course of his love for Anne, and he realizes that he had handed her over to Willie Stark, that "my nobility (or whatever it was) had had in my world almost as direct a consequence as Cass Mastern's sin had had in his." Lying there, contemplating the results of his idealism, he bitterly tells himself, "That was why I had got into my car and headed west, because when you don't like it where you are you always go west. We have always gone west." He sees the panorama of the conquest of the continent and he experiences a disillusionment even more thoroughgoing and complete than that which Nick Carraway had felt standing on the Atlantic shore.

> . . . . after you have built cabins and cities and bridged rivers, after you have lain with women and scattered children like millet seed in a high wind, after you have composed resonant documents, made noble speeches, and bathed your arms in blood to the elbows . . . . That is where you come, to lie alone on a bed in a hotel room in Long Beach, California.

It is in the West, after experiencing this disillusionment, that Jack discovers the dream of The Great Twitch, which for a time is able to absolve him of his complicit guilt, but which is not the end of his knowledge. He cannot believe in the green dream of the West, which finally ends only in the neon lights of Long Beach, California; but neither can he ultimately rest in the disillusioned cynicism resulting from the withering of that dream. Finally, Jack Burden, the student of history, comes to realize that, "History is blind, but man is not," but he also comes to realize that one must accept history, one must accept the burden of the past. For if one "could not accept the past and its burden there was no future, for without one there cannot be the other, and how if you could accept the past you might hope for the future, for only out of the past can you make the future."

The action of *World Enough and Time*, as in *Brother to Dragons*, takes place in Kentucky in the early years of the nineteenth century. But it, too, is not a story of a virgin land and its virtuous husbandmen and statesmen; it is rather a tale of "pride, passion, agony, and bemused aspiration." Central Kentucky at the time of the story was not a wilderness, but it was a land on the fringe of the wilderness, and Warren suggests that the land itself might be responsible for the tragedy of Jeremiah and Rachel.

> It was a violent and lonely land . . . . The people had come here to stay, and they would stay. They would possess the wild land, but the wild land possessed them too, and in a secret, ritualistic gluttony they had eaten the heart of every savage killed at the edge of the clearing or in the ambush by the ford . . . . It was a land of the fiddle and whiskey, sweat and prayer, pride and depravity.

That land could never be classed as a garden. And Warren suggests that "perhaps the land and the history of that land devised Jeremiah Beaumont and the drama in which he played, and the scene is the action and speaks through the mouth of Jeremiah Beaumont as through a mask." However, in the end, I do not think that Warren's villain is the land, as has been stated by one critic. For, really, the land is not malevolent, it is indifferent. As Rachel stands "sweating under the hot sun, in the middle of the brutal, vibrant, tumescent land," she is aware of the land drowsing and throbbing and brooding with its own secret, but she knows that it "cared nothing for her or her secret." Essentially, the land is the same Kentucky that provided the background for *Night Rider*. As Jeremiah realizes during his flight west with Rachel, "the land is the same, and its beauty, and is voiceless, whatever our errand, whether for wealth or peace, to open or close."

Warren quite explicitly examines and rejects the myth of the garden of primitive wilderness in this novel. After Jeremiah and Rachel are delivered from jail, they flee West, to the "last outpost in the swampy wilderness." They do not come to any wilderness eden, though, but to the swampy, malaria-ridden hangout of the river pirate band of the Grand Boz, the embodied symbol of evil and degradation. Jeremiah does find a "kind of peace" there in the wilderness, but one which he finally called the "black inwardness and womb of the quagmire."

> It was a peace with no past and no future, the absoluteness of the single, separate, dark massive moment that swells up fatly like a bubble from the deep mud, exists as a globe of slick film housing its noxious gas, then pops and is gone, and then with the regularity of the pulse of the blood, is followed by another that goes, and then another, forever.

And, just as he finds a certain peace, he also is able to find a certain kind of democracy, the democracy of the state of nature. He can sit and drink with men of the place from the common jug which made them all the same and was "their bond and communion." He can lay with one of the women of the place and find a "surer communion with them all than he had found in the drink from the jug lipped by every mouth." He finally obtains syphilis from the woman and, looking at the sore, says, "Let me regard this canker with reverence and amaze, like a jewel fit for a royal diadem. It proclaims me one of them, and of their great descent."

Afterwards, though, on his journey back East, after his confession of "the first and last temptation, to name the idea as all, which I did, and in that error was my arrogance, and the beginning of my undoing and cold exile from man," he also admits that he had fled West "to seek communion only in the blank cup of nature, and innocence there." But Jeremiah finds that the innocence of nature can be of no avail to man.

> For I had sought innocence, and had fled into that brute wilderness where all is innocence, for all is the same in that darkness, and even the shameful canker is innocence. But that innocence is what man cannot endure and be man, and now I flee from innocence and toward my guilt, and bear my heart within me like a bleeding sore of self, as I bear the canker on my body. And if I can clasp my guilt, then both may become the marks of my triumph, as of my shame.

And it is Jeremiah's acceptance of his guilt, of the knowledge that "the crime for which I seek expiation is never lost. It is always there. It is unpardonable. It is the crime of self, the crime of life. It is I" which provides a compassionately negative answer to the tortured question with which Jeremiah closes his journal and Warren closes his novel, "Oh, was I worth nothing, and my agony? Was all for naught?"

It is the absence of idealization, the refusal to romanticize and sentimentalize the past, the willingness to examine the myths which have dominated American thought throughout our nationhood, which sets Warren apart from practically all other modern American writers. Warren has examined the myth of the garden of America, the myth of the primitive innocence of America — and found the myths not only inadequate, but essentially false. In the end, Warren insists that we must return to a by now largely abandoned view of human nature (a view which is perhaps also essentially myth, but a myth not doomed to betrayal), the view that man is brother to dragons, that he is guilty of "original sin." In Willie Stark's brutal words, "Man is conceived in sin and born in corruption and he passeth from the stink of the didie to the stench of the shroud. There is always something." And, as Sweetwater says in *At Heaven's Gate*, "There's something horrible in everybody, till they work it out. It looks like a man's got to boil the pus out."

It is perhaps difficult for us to accept the essential truths of the doctrine of original sin. But perhaps it is necessary for us to do so, in order that not only our democracy, but also our particular form of civilization may survive. We can no longer continue to think of our-

selves as "children of light" in a world of darkness. Reinhold Niebuhr has stated that, "The ironic elements in American history can
be overcome, in short, only if American idealism comes to terms with
the limits of all human striving, the fragmentariness of all historic
configurations of power, and the mixture of good and evil in all human virtue." And George F. Kennan has warned us that, "A nation
which excuses its own failures by the sacred untouchableness of its
own habits can excuse itself into complete disaster."

Robert Penn Warren asks us to accept the conditions of our
humanity, for we have, "Each, experienced what it is to be men./We
have lain on the bed and devised evil in the heart./We have stood in
the sunlight and named the bad thing good and the good thing bad."
It is only in such knowledge and in acceptance of the past and its
burden, not in idealizing it or rejecting it, that we can go, with Jack
and Anne Burden, "out of the house and go into the convulsion of
the world, out of history into history and the awful responsibility
of Time."

James Ruoff

Humpty Dumpty And
All the King's Men

Since the Pulitzer Prize novel *All the King's Men* is coming to be
recognized as the most comprehensive statement of Robert Penn
Warren's philosophy and art,[1] it might be worth while to remark
upon a very general misconception regarding the title of the novel.
Now, ordinarily, of course, a title is not a matter of any great significance, but in this case it is important because it constitutes a

---

Reprinted from *Twentieth Century Literature*, III (October, 1957), 128-34, by
permission of the journal.
[1] See James Magmer, "Robert Penn Warren's Quest for an Angel," *Catholic
World*, CLXXXIII (1956), 178-83; Robert White, "Robert Penn Warren and
the Myth of the Garden," *Faulkner Studies*, III (1954), 59-67; J. Letargeez,
"Robert Penn Warren's Views of History," *Revue des Langues Vivantes*, XXII
(1956), 533-43.

symbolic expression of some of the author's basic ideas. It is, in fact, a Pandora's box which opens up to reveal the profoundly spiritual nature of Warren's convictions about the broad themes of man and God; and once we have properly understood the title in its relation to the context of the novel, we shall be in a position to see exactly what the author intended when he remarked recently of *All the King's Men*: "The book . . . was never intended to be a book about politics. Politics merely provided the framework story in which the deeper concerns, whatever their final significance, might work themselves out."[2]

According to the generally accepted interpretation, "the King" in *All the King's Men* is the protagonist Willie Stark, an interpretation which derives from the fact Willie is governor of the state, a man the other characters in the novel refer to as "the Boss." "The King's Men," on the other hand, are assumed to be all the people who in one way or another serve the Boss — Jack Burden, Willie's research man; Tiny Duffy, the lieutenant governor; Sugar Boy, Willie's bodyguard, etc. Then, too, there are "the King's women," the mistresses of the governor's palace — Sadie Burke, Anne Stanton, Willie's wife Lucy. As tidy as this interpretation undoubtedly is, something more than a casual reading of the story will show Willie Stark was never intended to be "the King" in *All the King's Men*, and that the title of the novel has a meaning more significant than critics have hitherto realized.

There are a number of reasons why Willie Stark cannot be "the King" in *All the King's Men*. There is, first, the nursery rhyme from which the title was derived: Willie is Humpty Dumpty not "King." Like Humpty Dumpty, Willie "sat on a wall" when he rose to become governor and "had a great fall" when shot down by Adam Stanton. Willie is, like his legendary counterpart, a synthetic creation, a grotesque composite of the abstract needs of the people who have shaped him. As Warren has pointed out, Willie's "power was based on the fact that somehow he could vicariously fulfill the secret needs of the people about him."[3] Hence the principal characters in *All the King's Men*, like Mr. Munn in Warren's *Night Rider* (1939), attempt to find themselves by merging their identities with another person. In Willie Stark the people of the state satisfy their craving for justice — hence Willie's easy political slogan "Your need is my justice" — while to the narrator, Jack Burden, Willie fulfills Jack's need of a father, his need of the purpose and direction and decisive

---

[2] Introduction, *All the King's Men* (Modern Library, 1953), vi.
[3] Introduction, p. i.

authority which have been lacking in his aimless life. To Adam
Stanton, "the man of idea" who eventually destroys him, Willie
represents the concrete power to accomplish the idealistic, humanitarian good which Adam has dedicated his whole life to achieve. In
short, it is an obvious truism to say that to Sadie Burke, to Anne
Stanton — to virtually every character in the novel — Willie Stark
represents the fulfillment of some secret compulsion, some indige-
nous shortcoming or incompleteness, and in this sense, most of all,
Willie is Humpty Dumpty — an artificial composite of the needs
inherent in the society which has created him. After Willie's assassination Tiny Duffy performs the futile ritual of attempting to
put Humpty Dumpty "back together again" when he seeks to
employ Jack Burden, Sadie Burke, and Sugar Boy, Willie Stark's
political aides.

But if Willie Stark is Humpty Dumpty, who then is king? In view
of the nursery rhyme it is difficult to see how Willie can be Humpty
Dumpty and king, too. Part of a solution to our problem is to be
found in Warren's introduction to the Modern Library Edition,
where he states that in *All the King's Men* he tried to "avoid writing
a straight naturalistic novel, the kind of novel the material so readily
invited." By the phrase "straight naturalistic novel" Warren apparently intended the bleakly deterministic and materialistic novel
which portrays its characters as being merely biological organisms
attracted and repelled by hereditary or environmental forces over
which they have no control. As we shall see, the "material" of *All the
King's Men* "readily invited" a novel of this description, for there is
a temptation to think of Willie Stark as an ineluctable demi-urge
riding the beast of the people to their moral collapse while the rider
himself is pulled to destruction by a gloomy necessity. And yet one
of Warren's main problems in writing *All the King's Men* was, I
think, to avoid any implications of determinism, to establish a sure
balance between the fact of Willie's diabolic attraction for others
and the fact of their free wills; for it was essential to Warren's moral
purpose, to his whole concept of man, that his characters exercise
free will, that Willie Stark remain, after all, only Humpty Dumpty
and not king — not Necessity, not God. In Warren's teleology only
God is King, and we are all of us "all the King's men."

God is not only King but absolute monarch informing every
moment of life with His purposive Will, and this predestination,
which under Warren's hand becomes something quite different from
determinism of a theological order, is "the material" that "readily
invited" what Warren calls "the straight naturalistic novel," the
novel which, in the tradition of Zola and Crane and Dreiser, is

informed by biological necessitarianism and psychological behaviorism. This naturalistic tradition is emphatically repudiated in *All the King's Men* when determinism, a chief characteristic of "the straight naturalistic novel," is sardonically labeled "The Big Twitch" by Jack Burden, who abjures it as totally inadequate to explain the events that take place in the story. The philosophy Jack Burden does come to accept, however, is one which has to do with the enigmatic paradox of Christianity — the omnipotence of God and the moral responsibility of man. And if at the end of the novel Jack's acceptance of this view of life is not without some reservations, we must remember that the paradox is baffling, is one that derives not from a spontaneous rational acquiescence but from a hard discipline of faith.

If omnipotent God has power over everything, how can man be said to have responsibility for anything? *All the King's Men* confronts this question cautiously, with a full cognizance of the critical tensions created by Darwin, Marx, Freud, and the holocaust of two world wars. From these spirit-shattering, enervating experiences, we must preserve, Warren tells us, what is most distinctive, significant and compelling about man, his consciousness and spirituality. According to Warren, man has moral choice, lives in an "agony of will," but, paradoxically, he has no choice, no power whatever, in the consequences of his moral life. To put it another way, in Original Sin — which looms darkly in the background of all Warren's novels from *Night Rider* to *Band of Angels* — Adam and Eve devoured a fruit of agony when they ate of the Tree of the Knowledge of Good and Evil, for in that fatal act they took upon themselves the knowledge of what was right and wrong, and consequently the responsibility for their actions; but they were denied the divinity which Satan had promised them, the power to transcend time and perceive, as God perceives, the ultimate consequences of good and evil. (In Milton's *Paradise Lost*, for example, a travesty on those supernal powers promised to Adam and Eve by Satan is implicit when Michael comes to inform them of the Atonement, of the *real* consequences of the Fall which only God can know.)

Ironically, then, the Fall simultaneously gave man moral vision and struck him blind: it gave him an immediate, a priori knowledge of good and evil as it related to any moral decision, to any incoherent fact, but it left him blind to the ultimate purpose or direction or consequences of the fact. As an individual, he is the master of his soul in a moment of crucial moral decision; as a species, he is a pawn in a cosmic game the ultimate meaning or purpose of which he can never know. In *All the King's Men* Hugh Miller expresses the human viewpoint, indeed the only view man has capacity for, when he remarks at the end of the novel that "History is blind, but man is not."

This concept of history as a fleeting montage of seemingly purposeless causes and effects, of good and evil events so complex and confoundingly intermingled that man cannot perceive the *ultimate* good or evil of anything, is profoundly confirmed in *All the King's Men*. Several years before the story of Willie Stark unfolds, Judge Irwin accepted a bribe which Irwin's friend Jack Burden uncovers in one of his investigations as Willie Stark's research man. This bribe, a completely voluntary act, sets off a chain reaction of mediate causes and effects. First, her discovery that her father concealed Irwin's crime so disillusions Anne Stanton that she becomes Willie Stark's mistress, while her brother Adam so modifies his militant idealism that he agrees to accept Willie's offer of the directorship of the Willie Stark Memorial Hospital. When Adam learns of Anne's affair, he assassinates Willie. But Irwin's bribe has even more far-reaching consequences. Jack's discovery of the bribe leads to Irwin's suicide, to Jack's realization that Irwin is his real father, to a reconciliation of Jack and his estranged mother. Was Judge Irwin's crime an evil? Although Warren is neither a weak-headed immoralist nor a sentimental relativist, his answer remains ambiguous. For his crime Irwin suffers guilt, repentance, absolution by atonement, just as do the other characters, whose particular crimes have been the indirect result of Irwin's: Jack Burden for uncovering Irwin's bribe, Anne Stanton for her adulterous relationship with Willie, Sadie Burke for her malicious jealousy of Anne and betrayal of Willie, and Lucy Stark for her pride of virtue and weakness of mind. Irwin's crime is evil because it results in the destruction of Willie, of Adam, of Irwin himself, and yet it has the undeniably good effects of saving Mrs. Burden's soul, of uniting her with her son, of bringing together Anne and Jack, and finally — if the reader chooses to remain skeptical of Willie's deathbed assurance that "things might have been different" — of freeing the people of the state from the grip of an unscrupulous demagogue. Hence Judge Irwin's crime and its results confirm what Jack Burden describes as the "moral neutrality of history." As an isolated, incoherent fact it is evil, but as a part of history, as one stitch in a complex, variegated tapestry, it has shades of both good and evil.

Willie Stark expresses a profound truth when he insists throughout the novel that good must come from evil because "evil is all you have to work with," while Adam Stanton, the more conventionally "noble" of the two, lives a dangerous ereror when he arbitrarily separates people and events into moral categories. The point is made by Jack Burden at the conclusion of the story: "As a student of history, Jack Burden could see that Adam Stanton, whom he came to call the man of idea, and Willie Stark, whom he came to call the man of fact, were doomed to destroy each other, just as each was doomed to try to use the other and to yearn toward and try to become the other, because each was incomplete with the terrible division of their age."[4] Willie brings about his own destruction when he tries to be like Adam when, like "the man of idea" that he is not, he sets out to create something which is completely devoid of evil. Inconsistent with his own philosophy that any good there is must come from evil, Willie dreams of building a magnificent hospital that will stand as the purely good achievement of his political administration, and yet, unknown to Willie, the hospital is tainted by evil in the moment of its conception, for the idea of the hospital is really the result of Willie's unconscious effort to compensate for the guilt he feels in protecting from prosecution his corrupt state auditor, Byram B. White. The hospital becomes an instrument of Willie's downfall when he refuses to permit the venal Gummy Larson from having the contract to construct it, when he refuses, in other words, to allow the good he dreams of achieving to be contaminated by evil, and this refusal prompts Tiny Duffy to inform Adam of Willie's affair with Anne. In shooting Willie Stark, Adam becomes himself "the man of fact," acknowledging Willie's dictum that the end justifies the means, but more than that, he proclaims by his act that he has God's knowledge, a final knowledge of good and evil. In his arrogant effort to usurp divinity, Adam repeats the folly of the Fall.

The fact that Willie's hospital is never built underscores man's tragic limitations. Confined to a tenuous reality of isolated facts, hemmed in by illusory absolutes of good and evil, man cannot perceive the transcendent reality, the ultimate moral purpose and direc-

---

[4] Page 462. In a recent article, Norman Kelvin argues that there is no basis for Warren's distinction between Willie as "the man of fact" and Adam Stanton as "the man of idea": The Willie Stark we met in the novel was as much a man of ideas as was the puritanical, compulsive Dr. Stanton. They merely held to *different* ideas, and while some of Willie's were outrageous, so were some of Adam's." But this appears to be a very literal reading of what, after all, is only a pair of arbitrary metaphors. It matters not, really, what phrases Warren employs to describe Willie and Adam so long as we recognize his meaning.

tion of life. Willie, "the man of fact," thinks he knows how things really are, and Adam Stanton, "the man of idea," thinks he knows how things ought to be, but both are incomplete, both presumptuous. So man lives on one moral level of reality, where he suffers an "agony of will," of personal responsibility, and God exists on another, the level of "history" or "direction," a level unknown to man, who yearns toward the fulfillment of some ideal good which in the "moral neutrality of history" has no objective existence. [5] On God's level, good and evil are not as inseparable as man persists in making them. What man conceives as a completed moral action is, in God's omniscient comprehension, merely another phase in man's continuous struggle to create some good in a fallen world he only faintly understands. Warren's concept of man as a fallen, debased, limited, and therefore heroic, creature working out moral decisions in an "agony of will" yet oblivious to the eventual good or evil of those decisions is one which recalls St. Augustine and medieval nominalists like Duns Scotus (the analogues of Warren's Puritanism), who stressed God's awful power and mystery, and man's irrationality and impotence. Like these medieval nominalists who reacted against the liberal rationalism of the Scholastics, Warren has repudiated the optimistic rationalism of the liberal reformers, just as he has repudiated their scientism and materialism — what Jack Burden refers to as "the dream of our age."

In *All the King's Men* man finds solace not in the liberal experience, not in the nineteenth-century dream of power through reason, but in the more ancient Christian experience of humility, repentance and hope; for Warren sees this world as a Dantesque purgatory where man works out his salvation by a process of transgression, acknowledgement of guilt, and contrition. Every character in *All the King's Men* who is worth saving eventually submits to this tortuous ritual of life: Cass Mastern, Judge Irwin, Willie Stark, Jack Burden, Mrs. Burden, Sadie Burke, and Anne Stanton. Tiny Duffy, like his friend Gummy Larson, is a mere shade, an abstraction, while Adam Stanton, paradoxically the "noblest" character in the novel, is, by the fact of his fierce and intransigent pride in virtue, quite beyond all hope of redemption. For the remainder of the characters in *All the*

---

[5] In a very interesting article ("The Meaning of Robert Penn Warren's Novels," *Kenyon Review*, X [Summer, 1948], 417), Eric Bentley describes Warren as "utterly empirical." This is of course true; nevertheless, Professor Bentley does not appear to be sufficiently aware of how in Warren's novels the facts of experience and Christian orthodoxy coalesce. Of how, in other words, empiricism confirms Warren's essentially Christian philosophy of life.

King's Men, however, the epigraph to the novel applies. Appropriately, the epigraph to *All the King's Men* is Manfred's tortured cry of hope in Canto III of Dante's *Purgatorio*: "Mentre che la speranze ha fior del verde."

As if to turn back to the end of the novel to interpret his story, Warren spells out these ideas about God and man in a religious tract dictated to Jack by Ellis Burden:[6]

> The creation of man whom God in His foreknowledge knew doomed to sin was an awful index of God's omnipotence. For it would have been a thing of trifling and contemptible ease for Perfection to create mere perfection. To do so would, to speak truth, be not creation but extension. Separateness is identity and the only way for God to create, truly create, man was to make him separate from God Himself, and to be separate from God is to be sinful. The creation of evil is therefore the index of God's glory and His power. But by His help. By His help and in His wisdom.

Jack Burden tentatively concurs in Ellis Burden's credo, "I did so to keep his mind untroubled," he says, "but later I was not certain that in my own way I did not believe what he had said." Jack's statement, although not an unqualified affirmation, is nevertheless a long step away from his earlier cynicism and philosophical determinism. It signifies a gradual awakening of Jack's spirituality, the beginning of an unconscious application of Cass Mastern's story to his own tragic experience in life. In his diary, which Jack had studied but could not understand until his own experiences confirmed its views, Cass Mastern had written: "I do not question the Justice of God, that others have suffered for my sin, for it may be that only by the suffering of the innocent does God affirm that men are brothers in His Holy Name." Cass Mastern sees the world as a vast spider web of intersecting lives: "Your happy foot or your gay wing may have brushed it ever so lightly, but what happens always happens and there is the spider, bearded black and with his great faceted eyes glittering like mirrors in the sun, or *like God's eye*, and the fangs dripping" (italics mine).

---

[6] I am not suggesting that Ellis Burden is a mouthpiece through which Warren expresses his views, nor that this religious tract is a violation of the novel's dramatic integrity. Ellis Burden is a fully developed, integrated character, and his tract does have a certain dramatic inevitability. Nevertheless, Ellis Burden and, to a less extent perhaps, Hugh Miller function in a way reminiscent of a Sophoclean chorus: they may have their etiology in Warren's pseudo-Greek drama *Proud Flesh*, which, written in 1938, was the germinal beginning of *All the King's Men*.

Because the Cass Mastern episode was printed as an independent story before the publication of *All the King's Men,* some critics have been quick to regard it as an extraneous feature, as a brilliant but irrelevant *tour de force,* and yet, as Eric Bentley has pointed out, it is really Warren's effort to "put the whole theme of a work into one short and strongly symbolic interlude."[7] It supplies not only an inverted contrast to Jack's own story, a contrast between a crime of commission and one of omission, but plainly underlines the dominant themes of the omnipotence of God, and the utter helplessness and brotherhood of men. Cass Mastern tripped the gossamer threads of the spider web when he seduced his best friend's wife: Judge Irwin when he accepted the bribe; Willie Stark when he refrained from prosecuting Byram B. White; and Jack Burden when he revealed the truth about Irwin. That Jack comes to accept Cass Mastern's view of the world is suggested when he observes toward the end of the story that "each of us is the son of a million fathers," but more pointedly, when Jack, who has always been lashed by a compulsion to seek and reveal the truth, tells his mother an outright lie rather than impart to her the cause of Irwin's suicide, and when he lies to Sugar Boy rather than name the man who was indirectly responsible for Willie Stark's death. On both occasions Jack's prevarication, like Marlow's lie to Kurtz's Intended in Conrad's *Heart of Darkness,* is an honest man's acknowledgement and atonement. Now sharing Cass Mastern's vision of the world as a web of humanity, Jack dares not assume responsibility for awakening the drowsy spider. He has come to see the brotherhood of men and the universality of guilt.

To assume, then, that Willie Stark is "the King" in *All the King's Men* is to ignore the meaningful symbolism of the title, to lose sight of Warren's basic idea. As I have attempted to show, *All the King's Men* portrays a world which Willie could not have ruled; for in that world of Warren's thoughtful creation there is but one King and we are all of us "all the King's men." From first to last, Willie Stark is but Humpty Dumpty, whose fall is a form of triumph for those who

---

[7] "The Meaning of Robert Penn Warren's Novels," 415-16. It ought to be mentioned, however, that the Cass Mastern episode is not completely successful. For one thing, it invites comparison with the adulterous relationship between Irwin and Mrs. Burden rather than with the Platonic romance of Jack and Anne. Hence at the end of the novel Warren felt it necessary to have Jack Burden point out that Judge Irwin bears no resemblance to Cass Mastern: "For Judge Irwin and Cass Mastern do not resemble each other very closely. If Judge Irwin resembles any Mastern it is Gilbert, the granite-headed brother of Cass" (p. 464).

survive him. As Ellis Burden states in another context, "Separateness is identity," and with the death of Willie those who involved their identities in him must find completion within themselves or not at all. As in any great tragedy, there is loss, there is gain: they have lost Willie but have gained the power to find themselves. It may not be a coincidence, therefore, that the conclusion to *All the King's Men* is reminiscent of the ending to another great tragedy as Jack Burden and Anne Stanton, like Adam and Eve departing from the Garden after the Fall, prepare to leave Burden's Landing forever to "go into the convulsion of the world, out of history into history and the awful responsibility of Time."